THE MAGIC

For a complete list of Management Books 2000 titles,
visit our web-site on http://www.mb2000.com

THE
MAGIC
OF
WORK

How you can balance your
Soul Work and Salary Work

Mike Pegg

2000

First published in 2002 by Management Books 2000 Ltd
Forge House, Limes Road
Kemble, Cirencester
Gloucestershire, GL7 6AD, UK
Tel: 0044 (0) 1285 771441/2
Fax: 0044 (0) 1285 771055
E-mail: m.b.2000@virgin.net
Web: mb2000.com

Printed and bound in Great Britain by Biddles, Guildford

British Library Cataloguing in Publication Data is available

ISBN 1-85252-400-6

CONTENTS

THE
MAGIC
OF
WORK

*How you can balance your
soul work and salary work*

About the Author

Mike Pegg has been working as an encourager and mentor for the past 35 years. His clients include Microsoft, Sony and The Dorchester Hotel. Leaving school at 15, Mike worked in a factory for six years. He then found the opportunity to do full-time voluntary work with mentally handicapped children. This led to his running therapeutic communities for disturbed young people and also teaching family therapy. Finally, he got to university but left after one year to set up his own business. During the 1970s, Mike began running programmes on Strengths Building. As a result, he was invited to educate leaders in business and sports. He now specialises in working with Pacesetters – people, teams and organisations that aim to take the lead and extend the lead. Mike has also done considerable work in helping people to build Super Teams. A prolific author, his books include *The Positive Planet*, *The Art of Mentoring* and *The Magic of Work*.

He can be reached at **mike@theartofmentoring.com**

INTRODUCTION

THE
MAGIC
OF
WORK

How you can balance your
Soul Work and Salary Work

INTRODUCTION

People want three things from work: **money, meaning and magic**. Money feeds the stomach; but meaning and magic feed the spirit and the soul. How can you do soul work and get paid a salary? How can you balance your finances and fulfilment? This book explores one of life's greatest adventures: how to find, follow and fulfil your **vocation**.

'I want to take more charge of my professional life,' you may say, 'but does that mean I have to go self-employed? Isn't that too risky? Is it possible to do work I love within a company?'

Great employers will always want great contributors. Perform superb work and help your sponsor to succeed, but still think like a freelancer. Stay in charge of your destiny because there are no safe jobs any more. Future businesses will want two kinds of players: 'Soul Players' and 'Star Players'. (They will have little time for 'Semi-Detached' Players.) Soul Players embody the spirit of the company and deliver consistent performances. Star Players also live the spirit, but use their talents to add that 'little bit extra'. Pacesetting organisations are now taking steps to retain such people. They are encouraging them to craft fulfilling roles that benefit both themselves and the business. Stay ahead of the game: make sure you take initiatives, rather than become institutionalised. Great employers will continue to want people who produce great work.

There are many ways to climb a mountain. Similarly, there are many roads you can travel towards doing satisfying work. Sometimes this calls for being both soul-wise and street-wise. The following pages outline three steps you may wish to consider.

Step One: VOCATION

Your vocation is your calling. It is what you are here to do. Sometimes people discover their purpose early in life, sometimes in later years. Values form the wellspring for your vocation, which may be expressed in a recurring life-theme. For example, the 'red thread' in your life might be: encouraging people; inventing products; building businesses; solving problems; creating beauty; making the world a better place – or whatever. The first chapter explores how to clarify your vocation. It looks at your Soul Work, Strengths, Style and Special Contribution. While your purpose will probably remain constant, the way you express it will change over the years. This brings us to the next step.

Step Two: VEHICLES

You may employ different vehicles for expressing your vocation during different stages of your life. How to choose the right vehicle? Bear in mind two factors. First, choose a 'Field' of work that you find fascinating. One in which you feel at ease yet are also able to excel. For example, You may feel 'at home' working with technology, business, science, sport, the arts, people management or whatever. Second, choose a 'Form' of work that fits your personality. For example, you may prefer to work as an individual, be a team member, run a business or whatever. Unfortunately some people fall in love with the vehicle – such as achieving status in a company – and forget their vocation. Anybody can do work they love; the art is getting somebody to pay you for it. The second chapter focuses on your Sponsors, Specific Goals, Superb Work and Support. This takes us onto the final step.

Step Three: VALUABLE WORK

People like to do worthwhile work and leave a legacy. Sometimes they only move onto the latter stage after achieving their original picture of 'success'. Why? They embarked on their professional lives aiming to achieve an 'external purpose', such as gaining riches or climbing the corporate ladder. Later in life, however, they focus on an 'inner purpose'. They concentrate on 'doing what they were meant to

Following your vocation

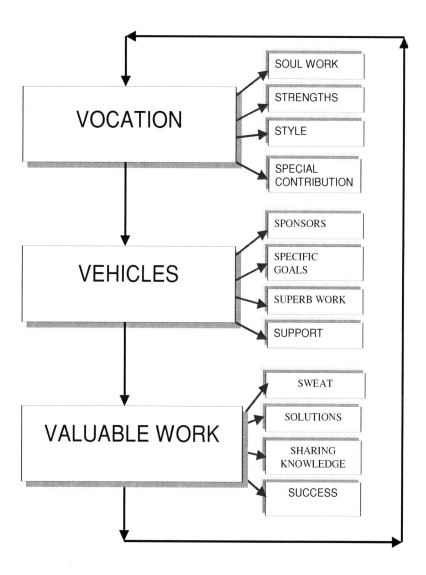

do.' As they grow older, people also find ways to pass on their wisdom. They may act as a positive model, be a mentor or find other ways to share their knowledge. The third chapter highlights the steps people take to fulfil these goals. It focuses on Sweat, Solutions, Sharing Knowledge and Success.

How to use *The Magic Of Work*? One option is to apply the tools when developing your talents. Another is to employ them to encourage other people when you are, for example, conducting a one-to-one session or workshop on Career Mentoring. For this reason, the book is written in the form of a conversation, providing many trigger questions. Some topics overlap, but take the ideas you like and integrate them with your own answers. If you wish, start with the introductory exercise called *A Sense Of Vocation*. When do you experience this sensation? Perhaps you are designing a product, solving a maths problem or totally absorbed in some other activity. The following pages focus on how to fulfil your vocation. They provide tools for pursuing your mission whilst also paying the mortgage. Enjoy the journey.

A SENSE OF VOCATION

The times that I experience a sense of vocation are:

●   When I am _____

_____

_____

●   When I am _____

_____

_____

●   When I am _____

_____

_____

STEP ONE
VOCATION
Finding Your Vocation

THE
MAGIC
OF
WORK

How you can balance your
Soul Work and Salary Work

Introduction

> ## POSITION WANTED
>
> **Where I am able:**
>
> - to build on my strengths
> - to work with soul mates
> - to do great work that helps my sponsors to be successful
> - to balance my finances and fulfilment
> - to make a positive contribution to the planet.

Where can you find such a job? Don't expect to see the role advertised in the newspapers. You will probably have to invent it. The challenge is – do you make the move proactively or wait until threatened by a crisis?

'My "wake-up call" came when my wife fell ill,' said Mark, who worked in high-tech company. 'On the surface, my 30s were successful years. Promotion followed promotion, but something kept nagging me. Years spent in "Strategic Meetings" with senior colleagues sapped my energy. I yearned to return to work that gave me a buzz.'

'My wife recovered after three months, but the trauma forced us to assess our priorities. We decided to turn away from the religion of "More", getting *more* income, *more* possessions. Pouring money into private education was not equipping our kids for the future world of work. So we began introducing them to positive models, enthusiastic people who were doing work they loved. Our children are very different, but each now feels more supported in pursuing their individual interests.'

'My wife started her own interior design business, but my career proved more problematic. 'You seem to have lost your ambition,' said the Managing Director, who planned to send me abroad before taking over his role. Leaving the company seemed the only alternative, until I spotted a gap in the market. Presenting a business plan to the Board, plus two firm orders from customers, I got the go-ahead to set up a new venture. Now I lead a small group of "believers" who run a pioneering business that produces a profit. I have returned to doing what I do best, developing software that makes a real difference.'

Near-death experiences focus the mind, we are told. Crises encourage us to examine our priorities. But we do not have to wait for thunderbolts to strike. Many people are now taking 'time out' to gain a greater perspective on their lives. Why? Individuals used to go on religious retreats. Nowadays, in the hustle and bustle of modern life, they find other ways to get an overview of their options. People recognise the need to make good quality decisions about their future direction.

How to start this process? This first chapter provides exercises you can use to find your vocation. Getting an overview is crucial, so we begin with *Setting The Scene*. The next step is to focus on your *Soul Work*, which is followed by identifying your *Strengths*. Looking back on the satisfying projects in your life, we then explore your successful *Style*. Finally, we focus on your *Special Contribution*. Let's begin with the big picture.

Setting the scene

'Start from your destination and work backwards.' Sages give this advice if we are planning a journey, embarking on strategic planning or considering our life goals. Throughout history, people have asked the eternal questions: Who am I? Where am I going? How do I get there? Some people are now adding more questions, such as: How can

I do fulfilling work? How can I make my best contribution? How can I build a better world? Here are some steps you can take when considering your aims.

You can clarify your Soul Work & Salary Work

Start by exploring where you are now. Try tackling the exercise called *Soul Work & Salary Work*. When do you feel you are doing soul work? When are you doing salary work? How can you do more soul work and, if possible, get some funding? (We will return to this topic later.) The second exercise on this theme is called *My Element*. Have you ever heard somebody say: 'I was in my element?' Describe the activities where you feel at ease and yet also able to excel. Doing soul work may be satisfying, but people also want to gain a sense of achievement, which takes us to the next step.

You can clarify your picture of success

People are different and want different things in life. Here are two exercises on this theme. The first one is called *Success*. Imagine that, in later years, you are looking back at your contribution. What will you have done that will mean your life has been successful? Move onto the exercise called *My Legacy*. People often want to leave behind something valuable. Reflecting back over the years, perhaps they want to have given their children a good start; created beautiful products; or helped to build a better world. What do you want to be your legacy?

SOUL WORK & SALARY WORK

SOUL WORK
The work I do that feels like <u>soul work</u> is:

- _____
- _____
- _____

SALARY WORK
The work I do that feels like <u>salary work</u> is:

- _____
- _____
- _____

SOUL WORK IN THE FUTURE
The specific steps I can take to do more soul work – <u>and</u> get paid a salary – in the future are:

- _____
- _____
- _____

MY ELEMENT

How can you do extraordinary work? One way is to ask yourself: 'When do I feel in my element?' Look for the activities where you feel at ease and yet also excel.

ELEMENT
The situation where I feel in my element is:

- When I _____

_____

EXCELLENCE
The steps I take to do excellent work when I am in my element are:

- _____

- _____

- _____

EXPANDING MY ELEMENT
The steps I can take to expand this kind of work are:

- _____

- _____

- _____

SUCCESS

People have different pictures of success. Imagine that, in later years, you are looking back over your life. Describe what you will have done that will mean you consider your life has been successful.

I will consider my life has been successful if:

● _____

_____

_____

● _____

_____

_____

● _____

_____

_____

MY LEGACY

The specific things I want to give people are:

1. _____

_____

_____

2. _____

_____

_____

3. _____

_____

_____

You can clarify your view of wealth

What do you mean by 'Wealth'? Is it being rich? Or is it being healthy, enjoying loving relationships and having the resources to harness your talents? Perhaps it is a mixture of all these elements. When somebody says: 'I want to win the lottery,' they may yearn for lots of money. On the other hand, they may simply long for the freedom to say: 'I want to be able to do what I want when I want.' The *My Wealth* exercise invites you to go through the following steps.

First: Describe your view of Wealth.
Second: Describe the Wealth you have at the moment.
Third: Describe the Wealth you would like in the future.
Fourth: Describe what you want to do with your Wealth.

You can clarify your purpose

'When I got there, there wasn't there.' People sometimes say this after journeying to a famous city, only to find that, because the city was so spread out, there was no real centre. Other people make this comment after striving to realise a vision of happiness. They spend years labouring to achieve an 'External Purpose', such as climbing the promotion ladder or stockpiling a pension. But reaching the target does not always bring contentment. After achieving their original aim, they explore their 'Internal Purpose', searching for a deeper sense of fulfillment.

The following pages offer three exercises on this theme, starting with *My Guaranteed Income*. Imagine you had a guaranteed income for the rest of your life. After taking holidays and giving away money, what would you do? The second is called *My Ideal Life*. Draw or describe your ideal life. What would you be doing? Where would you be living? How would you spend your days? What would be your picture of perfection?

Finally, try tackling the exercise called *My Purpose*. Bearing in mind your answers to the previous questions: What do you think you are here to do? Describe what you see as your purpose on the planet.

You can aim to be 'The Best In Your Class'

Every person has their own unique gifts. Mozart was not Beethoven; Mary Robinson was not Betty Boothroyd; Martin Luther King was not Desmond Tutu. Every person has his or her own colour to add to the paint box. Stretching ourselves, we can strive to be the best we can be. Some people neglect their talents by falling into the trap of negatively comparing themselves with others, saying: 'If I can't be Number One, there is no point in my participating in the activity.' James Fixx, author of *The Book of Running*, described a remedy for this disease. He told a story which, roughly translated, goes:

> A 35 year-old doctor – who had blond hair, glasses and two children – spent six months training to run in the New York Marathon. When the great day arrived he finished number 999 in a field of 1000 runners.
>
> When he returned to work on Monday, his fellow doctors asked him where he had finished in the race, so he told them. They teased him by saying: 'You trained for six months and only beat one person.' 'That doesn't matter,' he replied. 'I was best in my class.' They could not understand what he meant, so they asked: 'What class was that?'
>
> He explained: 'That was the class for 35 year-old doctors with blond hair, glasses and two children. There is no point in comparing myself with other people – that way I am always going to lose. I gave 100% and that is all I can ever do. I can only be the best person, runner or doctor I can be.'

You can clarify your present priorities

'Leaving the Career Review session, my long-term goals were crystal-clear, but then short-term events threw me off-course,' explained one person. Interruptions, pressures and other peoples' agendas force us onto the back foot. How to tackle the daily demands but also focus on the big picture? Here are several exercises on this theme.

What are your burning issues at the moment? When tackling the exercise called *My Top Priorities,* one person wrote: 'Caring for my 6-week-old son, who is suffering from a life-threatening illness. Supporting my family during the crisis. Handing over a project to my deputy and making sure he can guide it to success.' The answers he gave put his long-term career issues in perspective.

Daily events leave clutter, taking energy from our lives, so sometimes it is important to have a 'Spring Clean'. The *White Room* exercise invites you to take this step. Imagine your life is an empty, white room, containing nothing except your family. Starting afresh, you can put what you want into the room. List the 3 People, 3 Strengths, 3 Goals, 3 Possessions and 3 Other Things you would put in your White Room. Then take steps to concentrate on these energy-givers in your present life.

You can 'control the controllables'

'But I have strong control needs,' you may say. 'While I'm happy to take charge of my career, how do I minimise the risk?' Peak performers in any field – be it business, sports or the arts – focus on 'Controlling the Controllables.'

Imagine you are competing in the Olympic 100 meters final. You can control your attitude, preparation, self-talk and concentration. You can't control the weather, the crowd, the times clocked by other athletes. Channel energy into doing your personal best, rather than worrying about what you can't influence.

My Controllables explores the theme of shaping your future. Looking at your life and work, describe three things.

1. **The things you can control.** For example, you can control your persistence, talent development, networking, etc.

2. **The things you can't control.** For example, you can't change other peoples' personalities, staid corporate cultures or the whole world.

3. Plan how to **build on what you can control** and **manage what you can't control**. As somebody said: 'You don't choose your talent, but you do choose what to do with your talent.'

Time to move on. Having got the big picture, we can now take other steps towards exploring your vocation. The first stage will be to focus on your *Soul Work*.

WEALTH

WEALTH
My definition of wealth is:

● _____

PRESENT WEALTH
The wealth I have at the moment is:

● _____

● _____

● _____

FUTURE WEALTH
The wealth I want to have in the future is:

● _____

● _____

● _____

MAKING USE OF WEALTH
The specific things I want to do with the wealth are:

● _____

● _____

● _____

MY GUARANTEED INCOME

This exercise invites you to focus on some of the deepest drivers in your life. If you had a guaranteed income for the rest of your life, what would you do? You might go around the world, have holidays and give money to other people. But then what would you do?

If I had a guaranteed income for the rest of my life, I would:

● _____

_____

_____

● _____

_____

_____

● _____

_____

_____

MY IDEAL LIFE

What would be your ideal life? Use this page to draw and describe your ideal life. Then focus on concrete steps you can take to make this happen.

My ideal life would be:

MY PURPOSE

My purpose on the planet is:

- _____

_____

- _____

_____

- _____

_____

My plans for pursuing my purpose on the planet are:

- To _____

_____

- To _____

_____

- To _____

_____

MY TOP PRIORITIES

My top three priorities in my life at the moment are:

- To _____

  _____

  _____

- To _____

  _____

  _____

- To _____

  _____

  _____

MY WHITE ROOM

Sometimes it is important to have a 'Spring Clean' to sort-out our lives. We can then refocus on the things that are really important to us. The White Room exercise invites you go through this process. Imagine your life is an empty, white room with nothing in it except your family. Starting afresh, you can put what you want in your White Room. List the three people, three strengths, three goals, three possessions and three other things you would put in your White Room. Then take steps to concentrate on these energy-givers in your present life.

The three people:

- _____

- _____

- _____

The three strengths:

- _____

- _____

- _____

The three goals:

- _____

- _____

- _____

The three possessions:

- _____

- _____

- _____

The three other things:

- _____

- _____

- _____

MY CONTROLLABLES

Peak performers focus on what they can control in their lives and work. This exercise invites you to do three things. First: describe the thing you can control. Second: describe the things you can't control. Third: describe the specific things you can do to build on what you can control and manage what you can't control.

CAN CONTROL
The things I <u>can control</u> in my life and work are:

● I can control _____

_____

● I can control _____

_____

● I can control _____

_____

● I can control _____

_____

● I can control _____

_____

CAN'T CONTROL
The things I <u>can't control</u> in my life and work are:

● I can't control _____

● I can't control _____

● I can't control _____

MY CONTROLLABLES - Action Plan
The specific things I can do to build on what I can control, and manage what I can't control, are:

● I can _____

_____

_____

● I can _____

_____

_____

● I can _____

_____

_____

Soul Work

'Sometimes you choose your calling. More often your calling chooses you,' is the maxim. How to recognise your calling? Many clues are contained in your soul work. When do you feel completely engaged in an activity? When, for you, does time go away? Our work is one of our greatest companions. You may have at least three kinds of soul mates in life:

- your life-partner
- your vocational soul mates – the people with whom, when it comes to work, you have a values-fit
- your work – people often find their 'spiritual home' when putting their heart into their vocation.

Here are some steps to consider along the way.

You can identify your soul work

When do you feel most creative? When do you get your adrenalin highs? Try tackling the exercise called *Time Goes Away*. Describe the activities where you feel completely absorbed and carried away. Are there any themes in these activities? If so, how can you build on them? Here are some answers other people gave when describing such experiences:

> Time goes away for me when I am ... designing a building ... creating a new dish for diners in my restaurant ... singing an aria to a packed auditorium ... navigating how our business team can get from A to Z ... playing football for my Premiership club, because the pitch is the place where I really feel at home.

Two pioneering books also explore the concept of doing soul work. *Flow: The Psychology Of Optimal Experience*, by Mihalyi Csikszentmihalyi, provides fresh views on our creative moments.

Great performers develop the ability to flow, focus, finish and, as a by-product, find fulfilment. How can you follow this process in your way? Try tackling the exercise called *My Flow Experiences*. Describe when you have enjoyed a sense of flow. What were you doing right then? How can you follow these principles in the future?

Great work calls for harnessing your natural gifts. Sounds common sense, but sometimes it gets forgotten. *Now, Discover Your Strengths*, by Marcus Buckingham and Don Clifton shows how to develop your assets. When you are in your element, say the authors, you yearn to repeat the experience. Building on their ideas, try tackling the exercise called *I Can't Wait To Do This Again*. Which are the activities that, when you are involved in them, you can't wait to repeat in the future? These need not be world-changing events. You may enjoy a sense of peace when cooking a meal, writing an article or spending a day with loved ones. Try tackling the exercise called *Fulfilment*. Let's explore other ways to feed your gifts.

You can do the things that give you energy

'Two years ago I switched focus in my professional life,' said Janet, a research scientist. 'Why? One day I realised I had stopped doing inspiring work that made me feel alive. Being an Achiever, I started each day at 0 and aimed to get to 10. Satisfaction came from ticking off each task. But I had hit a problem. The tasks I was doing, and the people I worked alongside, no longer provided stimulation. Duty-driven, I drove myself to complete the jobs, but the outcome was sterile. Looking back at the end of each day, I felt exhausted but unsatisfied.'

'The solution? I tore up my career plan and switched to a more meaningful project, stepping off the formal promotion ladder. Spending time with interesting colleagues also gave me a kick. Scientific research can be lonely, but I have always liked mixing with creative friends. Several years of neglecting my network meant that I was out of touch, so it took time to rekindle relationships. Now I feel alive, stronger and enjoy my work.'

Energy is life – without it, we become lifeless. What gives you energy? What drains energy? Enthusiasm is priceless. When do you get excited and ecstatic? Try tackling the exercise on this theme. Challenging questions are posed by the next exercise called *Pleasure and Pain*. Looking at your life at the moment, what is the ratio of pleasure and pain? How much pain do you absorb before the alarm bells start ringing? Consider how to spend more time on the activities, and with the people, that give you positive energy.

You can work with vocational soul mates

People work best with kindred spirits. Who are your vocational soul mates? Who are the people with whom, when it comes to work, you have a values-fit? Keep in touch and, if possible, work with such people. Feeling 'at home' in their company, you start on Rung 5 of a 10 Rung Ladder. Knowing each other's strengths also removes uncertainty, so cooperating is not a 'blind date'. Building on common values makes it easier to agree on a shared vision and deliver visible results. Try tackling the exercise called *My Vocational Soul Mates*. Describe the steps you can take to build with such people, because maintaining these relationships will eventually produce job opportunities.

Soul work is crucial in ensuring that you feel true to yourself. Funding is more likely to follow, however, if you can make a brilliant contribution to a potential sponsor. Time to move onto the next step, clarifying your *Strengths*.

TIME GOES AWAY

The activities I get involved in when, for me, time goes away are:

- when I am _____

- when I am _____

- when I am _____

Some of the themes in these activities are:

- _____

- _____

- _____

Bearing these in mind, my vocation may be:

- _____

- _____

- _____

I CAN'T WAIT
TO DO THIS AGAIN

The times I experience the feeling 'I can't wait to do this again' are:

● when I am _____

_____

_____

● when I am _____

_____

_____

● when I am _____

_____

_____

MY FLOW EXPERIENCES

The time I had a flow experience was:

- when I _____

_____

The things I did right to create the flow experience were:

- I _____

- I _____

- I _____

The things I believe I can do to follow these principles in the future are:

- I can _____

- I can _____

- I can _____

FULFILMENT

The things I find fulfilling are:

- _____
- _____
- _____
- _____
- _____

The steps I can take to do more of these things I find fulfilling are:

- _____
- _____
- _____
- _____
- _____

ENERGY

The things that give me energy are:

- _____
- _____
- _____

The things that drain energy are:

- _____
- _____
- _____

The specific steps I can take to do more of the things that give me energy are:

- _____
- _____
- _____

PLEASURE AND PAIN

PLEASURE
The things that give me pleasure are:

● _____

● _____

● _____

PAIN
The things that give me pain are:

● _____

● _____

● _____

PLEASURE - MY ACTION PLAN
The steps I can take to build on those things that give me pleasure, and minimise those that give me pain, are:

● _____

● _____

● _____

MY VOCATIONAL SOUL MATES

The people with whom I have a values-fit concerning work are:

- _____
- _____
- _____
- _____
- _____
- _____

- _____
- _____
- _____
- _____
- _____
- _____

The specific things I can do to maintain contact and build with these people are:

- to _____
- to _____
- to _____

Strengths

John Lennon and Paul McCartney wrote and sang memorable songs. If you were the manager of The Beatles, you would ask them to sing lead vocals, rather than Ringo. David Beckham hits marvellous crosses from the right wing for Manchester United. If you were his manager, you would ask him to capitalise on this skill, rather than play left back. If you commissioned Pavarotti for a concert, you would ask him to sing, rather than do conjuring tricks. If you were leading a start-up business in a garage, you would ask everybody to use their best talents. Why? Because it gives you the greatest chance of success.

A rose can become a better rose; it cannot become a daffodil. People develop, they rarely change. Great performers do what they do best, do a few things and do these brilliantly. They also balance apparent contradictions. When performing superbly, for example, they picture the overall vision whilst also seeing the details. They are good finishers and deliver on their promises. Focusing on strengths does not mean that you ignore the 'fall out' from your weaknesses; it simply means that you find ways to compensate for them. World class performers are extremists – they make extreme use of their natural talents.

'But for years I was told to become an all-rounder,' remarked John, an IT contractor. 'My boss sent me to countless courses dedicated to 'improving' my weaknesses. Years later, I found myself far removed from my skill set. Redundancy acted like a wake-up call and I returned to my first love, which is trouble-shooting computer problems. Now I look forward to getting my hands dirty each day, rather than processing paper work or sitting in boring meetings.'

Antoine St. Exupery talked about the 'Murdered Mozart' within each person. Not everybody can be a Mozart, but everybody can nurture their gifts. Let's explore some of the steps towards making this happen.

You can clarify your super strengths

'My team members stared with blank faces when invited to say what they did well,' reported one manager. 'Strangely, they found it easier when asked to define their two or three 'Super Strengths.' Previously they found it hard to identify their talents, perhaps feeling they should be good at everything under the sun. Encouraging people to be selective got them to highlight the few things they did brilliantly.'

What are your top three talents? If you wish, tackle the exercise called *My Super Strengths*. Another option is to explore the exercise called *The MD's Question*. If you were a Managing Director, what would you hire yourself to deliver? Answering this forces you to concentrate on what you can 'guarantee' to an employer. The danger is, of course, that you might underestimate your potential. How to identify your special gifts? Here are some steps along the road.

You can clarify where you are 'Hands-on' and 'Helicoptering'

Brilliant performers do not fit the strait-jackets supplied by old-fashioned 'psychometric tests'. When the 'tester' asks: 'Are you a visionary or do you have attention to detail?' their answer is: 'Yes.' Why? When operating at their best, they balance apparent contradictions. Where does this happen for you? Where are you both 'Hands-On' and 'Helicoptering'? Try tackling the exercise on this theme. Clarify the activities where you simultaneously see both the overall vision and the minute details. Keep putting yourself into such situations, because these are where your gifts come into play.

MY SUPER STRENGTHS

My top three super strengths are:

- I can _____

_____

_____

- I can _____

_____

_____

- I can _____

_____

_____

THE MD QUESTION

If I was an MD, what would I hire myself to deliver?

The specific things I would hire myself to deliver would be:

1. to _____

_____

_____

2. to _____

_____

_____

3. to _____

_____

_____

HELICOPTERING

The situation where I am simultaneously able to be hands-on and to helicopter is:

● When I _____

_____

The things I do right in this situation is:

● I _____

● I _____

● I _____

The things I can do to put myself in more of these situations and build on these qualities are:

● I can _____

● I can _____

● I can _____

You can clarify where you have good personal radar

Al Siebert, writing in *The Survivor Personality*, explained that great performers possess 'Personal Radar'. When entering certain situations, they quickly see patterns and can predict 'what will happen before it happens.' Outstanding athletes, for example, always seem to be several moves ahead of the game. Footballers who might be relatively slow, but who demonstrate good positional play, are often described as: 'Having the first 10 yards inside their head.' Where do you have good Personal Radar? If you wish, try tackling the exercise on this theme.

'I have good radar when negotiating between two sides during a conflict,' explained a mediator. 'The logical road-blocks are obvious. The emotional roadblocks should be just as predictable, but sometimes they lie deep beneath the surface. I seem to be able to foresee, and often bypass, these blockages before they ruin our attempts at conflict resolution.'

'I have good radar when listening to new students,' reported a music teacher. 'Hearing them play for the first time, I project myself along the path that we must follow together. Within the first few minutes, I have rehearsed all the struggles they must go through in order to blossom. Returning to the present, I carefully talk with the student about the musical and personal challenges ahead. Then we agree on our plan for helping them to develop as a musician.'

Radar provides lots of information, but people must also develop the Repertoire to achieve Results. Great performers possess natural radar in their chosen field and this expands with experience over the years. They are also often hungry to learn fresh skills. Expanding their repertoire offers more tools and techniques that they can use for delivering the right results.

PERSONAL RADAR
Peak performers focus on their:

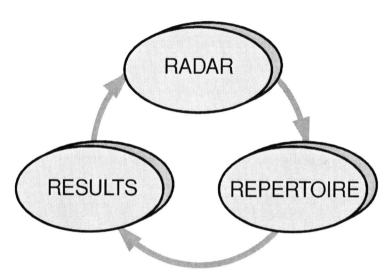

One footnote concerning Personal Radar. Great athletes seldom make fine coaches. Because they sum up situations quickly, they cannot understand why others fail to see what to them is blindingly obvious. One famous footballer turned manager, for example, ranted at his forwards for failing to score goals. He said: 'It is simple. All you do is hit the ball into the top left hand corner of the net.' Demonstrating this skill, he then hit five consecutive volleys into the roof of the net. Turning to the players, he asked: 'Why can't you do that during matches?' Superb coaches, on the other hand, have the radar of an educator. They know how to pass on knowledge in a way the learner can receive.

You can clarify where you make complicated things simple

'Cooking a meal for 500 people is relatively simple for me,' explained

Phil, a banqueting chef. 'Certainly my staff and I must do a lot of forward planning, but I enjoy the whole process. Sometimes I like the challenge of serving a new dish, because the adrenalin rush puts me on my mettle. Cooking for 500 might make some people nervous, but I have never considered it a problem. Everything has gone well so far, touch wood.' Let's not confuse 'simple' with 'easy'. Mastering an art makes the execution seem effortless, but this hides years of practice. Paradoxically, some potentially fine performers do not build on their true gift because they say: 'I tend to do it naturally, so I didn't think it was anything special.' Try tackling the exercise called *Making Complicated Things Simple*. Where are you able to make complex tasks seem straightforward? How can you develop this talent?

You can clarify where you quickly get 'pictures of perfection'

'Retail still sets my pulses racing,' said Karen, who runs three boutiques in London. 'As a child, I loved to visit the shops in our village – the greengrocer's, butcher's and the post office. In my mind's eye, I rearranged the goods to create the perfect shop. I still have that "feeling" for retail. When entering a shop, I immediately see how we can make better use of the "hot spots". Drawing customers into the shop comes next, followed by guiding them to certain goods. It only takes five minutes to see how the shop can be more profitable.'

Where do you experience this feeling? Perhaps you are facilitating a group, fixing a broken engine or landscaping a garden. Try tackling the exercise on this theme. Play to your strengths by putting yourself into places where you quickly get a picture of perfection.

You can clarify where you quickly see patterns

Great performers immediately search for patterns when entering their field of expertise. Scanning the situation, they collect information and select the right strategies for achieving success. Pattern Recognition is one of the clues to identifying your 'A' talents, rather than your 'B' or 'C' talents. Where do you quickly recognise patterns? What kind of patterns do you see? How can you build on these strengths?

Looking at my own working life, for example, I loved being a football manager, but only reached the level of Youth Development Officer. Why? When the teams kicked off, it took quite a time to work out what was happening on the field. When working with people in business, however, it was relatively straightforward to find their successful patterns. Football remains a passion, but my natural abilities lie in other fields.

You can clarify where you deliver peak performance beyond pressure

'Saturday will be wonderful,' proclaimed the Tenor. 'We will be singing Nessum Dorma to an audience of 500,000 million people around the world.' Looking forward to the opportunity, he felt ecstatic, rather than paralysed by fear. Outstanding athletes talk about 'Going into the Zone.' They say: 'I didn't feel pressure. The game slowed down. It was as if I had all the time in the world. It was as if I was playing a different kind of game.' They have achieved the athlete's Holy Grail. Events may be going slowly for them, but they proceed at breakneck pace for lesser mortals.

When do you feel calm, controlled and centred? When do you feel able to perform beyond pressure? When do you enter your equivalent of the Zone? Perhaps you are presenting to a high-powered group, making a sale or writing an article. What are the reasons that you feel calm? Try tackling the exercise on this theme. Building on strengths helps to clarify your offering to potential sponsors. But how do you work best? Let's explore the next step towards employing your talents.

MY PERSONAL RADAR

The place where I have good personal radar is:

- _____

The specific things I do right to use my radar well in that situation are:

- _____

- _____

- _____

The specific things I can do to capitalise on and make the best use of my radar in the future are:

- _____

- _____

- _____

MAKING COMPLICATED THINGS SIMPLE

MY TALENTS
The activities where I am able to make complicated things appear simple are:

- _____
- _____
- _____

MY TALENT DEVELOPMENT
The specific things I can do to build on these natural talents are:

- _____
- _____
- _____

PICTURES OF PERFECTION

PICTURES OF PERFECTION
The activities where I quickly see pictures of perfection are:

● When I am _____

_____

● When I am _____

_____

● When I am _____

_____

The specific things I can do to put myself in more of these situations and build on my talents are:

● I can _____

_____

● I can _____

_____

● I can _____

_____

PATTERN RECOGNITION

Peak performers have the ability to recognise patterns in their chosen field. They also have the repertoire to capitalise on this ability and achieve successful results. This exercise invites you to focus on where you have this ability to see patterns.

The situation where I see patterns is:

● _____

_____

The kinds of patterns I see are:

● _____

● _____

● _____

The steps I can take to build on my ability to see patterns in this situation are:

● _____

● _____

● _____

PEAK PERFORMANCE
BEYOND PRESSURE
Going into the zone

The activity where I perform well yet feel calm and free from pressure is:

● When I am _____

_____

The reasons I feel calm and free from pressure are:

● _____

● _____

● _____

The specific things I can do to keep developing my performance in these situations are:

● _____

● _____

● _____

Style

Everybody has a positive history. The organic approach to development concentrates on nurturing peoples' successful patterns; be they a golfer, dancer, painter, engineer or whatever. Revisiting the principles that worked for them in the past creates inner belief. People start believing in the gut. 'Be who you are, only more so,' is the motto. The tricky part is following similar paths in the future. While the principles may be eternal, the key is translating these into actions in a fast evolving world. Sometimes the seeds of our creative patterns began growing many years ago – so how to reap the harvest from this land of plenty?

You can clarify your successful style

Looking back on your life, what have been the most satisfying 'projects'? Perhaps you found it fulfilling to lead a rock group, travel around the world, renovate a house or whatever. Try tackling the exercise called *My Successful Style*. Start by considering your life over the decades: 0-10-20-30 and so on. Reflecting on each time span, describe the projects you found satisfying. Early in life, you may have pursued a hobby or acted in a drama group. Later in life, you may have launched a marketing campaign or produced a piece of software.

Time to explore deeper. Focusing on one particular project, try to answer the following questions. How did the project Start? How did you Seek Information? What were your Specific Goals? Did you do the project for yourself or for a certain kind of Sponsor? What was your actual working Style? How did you Solve Problems? What parts did you find most Satisfying? What for you made it Successful? Complete the answers for one project; then move onto another. Bearing the information in mind, can you identify any recurring themes?

'My pattern is staring me in the face, which means I must take some tough decisions,' said Geoff, the Vice President of an International Airline. 'I am an engineer. All my life I have got a kick from making things. When I was young, it was building model aeroplanes, later it was constructing Airport Terminals. The question is simple: Am I in the right job?'

'Looking back on my life, the pattern is clear. First, I decide to build something exciting. Then I soon get a vivid picture of the finished product, often in detail and Technicolor. Second, I find money to pursue the dream, either by financing it myself or getting hired by employers. Third, the brief does not change. If am being paid to construct a building, for example, the agreed design stays. Alterations may take place at the edges, but we stick to the overall vision. This is crucial.'

'Fourth, I get the best resources. As a child, I bought the best model equipment. As a Project Director, I hire the best experts from around the world. Fifth, I immerse myself completely in the day-to-day work. Leadership gurus say I must remain detached; but getting my hands dirty supplies the information needed to achieve the vision. Finally, the job gets finished: the model aeroplane flies; the Terminal opens to applause. It is beautiful and it works. Then it is time to create the next dream.'

Geoff outlined his challenge: 'My present job sounds great but, although I am the VP, I am far away from my successful pattern. Why? My Chairman founded the Airline and still sees the company as his baby. Every three months he parachutes a new vision into the HQ building, usually on a Monday morning. People are thrown into meetings, charged with discussing how to overcome barriers to reaching his fresh goal. Talk is endless, but we never deliver a finished product. Not to worry, in three months time he will produce another vision.' Geoff explored his options and eventually moved on to mastermind the construction of a new airport. He may no longer have the status, but he enjoys real satisfaction.

What is your successful style? Some people quickly identify their preferred method. Others discover that they have two differing approaches. One involves them working alone, such as when writing a book; another involves them working with people, such as when contributing to a team. The approach you adopt will depend on where you plan to apply your talents. Soul Work and Strengths define 'What' you can offer to potential employers. Style defines 'How' you work best. Time to define your *Special Contribution* to sponsors.

MY SUCCESSFUL STYLE

Start by listing satisfying projects at different stages of your life. Then focus on one of these ventures. You will be asked to answer some questions about the project. Later you will be invited to apply your findings. Let's start with an overview of things you have done in your life. (You may find it easier to start with ventures that have happened more recently, then work backwards.)

MY SATISFYING PROJECTS

The 'projects' that have been satisfying for me at different stages of my life have been:

0 ● _____

● _____

● _____

10 ● _____

● _____

● _____

20 ● _____

● _____

● _____

30 ● _____

● _____

● _____

40 ● _____

   ● _____

   ● _____

50 ● _____

   ● _____

   ● _____

60 ● _____

   ● _____

   ● _____

70 ● _____

   ● _____

   ● _____

80 ● _____

   ● _____

   ● _____

ONE PARTICULARLY
SATISFYING PROJECT

THE SATISFYING PROJECT - The project that you found satisfying, stimulating and, to your mind, successful, was:

- _____

STARTING UP - How did the project start? What happened to get you interested? Did you think of the idea yourself? Did somebody suggest the idea to you?

_____

_____

_____

STIMULATION - Many activities capture our interest, but only a few motivate us to translate thought into action. These questions ask you to go deeper into the real drivers. What was the stimulation that provided the kick-start? Did it come from within you, from elsewhere or from a combination of both? If the latter, what was the sequence of events? What did you see as the benefits of pursuing the project?

_____

_____

_____

SEEKING INFORMATION - How did you seek information about the project? Describe the actual steps you took to get a full picture.

_____

_____

_____

SPECIFIC GOALS - When you set out, did you have specific goals? If not, what were your aims? Did you set the goals yourself? Did other people set the goals for you? Was it a combination of both? If you did have goals, to what extent were they about achieving specific results? To what extent were they about achieving satisfaction?

_____

_____

_____

SPONSORS - Did you do the project just for yourself? Did you do it for a particular person or other sponsors? If you were working for a particular sponsor, what were the characteristics of that person?

_____

_____

_____

STYLE - Great performers often 'censor' what they actually do when they are working. Looking back, they give an idealised picture, missing out the daily mundane tasks, the mistakes and the real hard work. If I were watching you during the project, what would I see you actually doing? Describe this in great detail.

_____

_____

_____

SUPPORT - What encouragement did you receive? Did you get the support from within yourself, from outside or from both? Was it physical, practical, psychological or a combination of all three? What form did it take? What practical steps did you take to encourage yourself?

_____

_____

_____

SUPERB WORK - Did you do anything to add that 'little bit extra' to perform superb work? Describe in detail what you actually did to ensure you produced something special.

_____

_____

_____

SOLUTIONS - What challenges did you face on the journey towards achieving your goals? How did you go about solving these issues?

_____

_____

_____

SUCCESS - What happened that meant you felt successful about completing the project? Did you reach a specific goal? Describe what actually took place. What did you and other people say when looking back at the project?

_____

_____

_____

SATISFACTION - Finally, and most importantly, what were the things about the project that gave you the most satisfaction? Was it being involved in the process, gaining the prize or a combination of both? Which parts of the process were the most satisfying? How can you do more of these things in the future?

_____

_____

_____

MY SUCCESSFUL STYLE

THE APPLICATION

How to apply what you have learned? Here is a framework you may wish to follow. Building on some elements from previous exercises, it invites you to identify: (a) your strengths, (b) your successful style, (c) the specific benefits you could offer to a potential sponsor, (d) the potential sponsors who might be interested, and (e) the steps you can take to shape your future.

Strengths - my top three strengths are that I am able:

● to _____

● to _____

● to _____

Successful style - I believe that my successful style is:

● to _____

● to _____

● to _____

Bearing this in mind, the implications of my successful style are that it is important for me:

● to _____

● to _____

● to _____

Specific benefits - bearing in mind my strengths and my successful style, the specific benefits I could deliver to a potential sponsor are:

- to _____

- to _____

- to _____

Sponsors - the steps I can take to find such potential sponsors are:

- to _____

- to _____

- to _____

Shaping my future - the steps I can take to find or create a specific niche are:

- to _____

- to _____

- to _____

Special Contribution

Today is the age of 'the never satisfied customer.' They demand outstanding service, saying things like: 'I want this. I want it just for me. I want it NOW!' Sounds tough, but it offers opportunities. Today is also the age of the brilliant niche supplier. Providing they reach enough potential sponsors, there will always be a market for people who provide quality.

Helen has a gleam in her eye when describing her growing business. She aims to become a 'Proactive Vet'. Marvellous with animals, she is also good with people. She believes in 'treating the whole system', both the owner and the pet. 'Sometimes the owners need more help than the animal,' she explains, 'but you have to be careful how you pass on such advice.' One year after completing her training, Helen has found a boss who supports her brand of veterinary medicine.

'Today many people lead busy lives,' says Helen. 'They want to care for their animals, but also work long hours. The district where I practice is full of high achievers who have lots of money but little time. So I plan my visits around their schedules, often on weekends, rather than force them to fit into surgery hours. I travel to their homes to give animals Vaccination Boosters and a full examination. Before leaving, I make an appointment to return in 3 months time. People seem happy to pay for ongoing checks and preventive work with their animals.'

How did she find her 'boss'? Veterinary practices are often well established and rely on retaining their customers. Before graduating from college, Helen spent 18 months researching potential employers. She looked for somebody: a) who would be in tune with her treatment philosophy and; b) who did not have partners fighting to inherit the business. The breakthrough arrived when attending a workshop on pioneering methods of horse training. She met a vet who embraced a 'holistic' approach to animal treatment. After an initial trial placement, she relocated to join his practice. Helen is encouraged to develop her style of providing service to a new generation of customers.

How to clarify your unique offering? Again, ask yourself the following questions: 'What are my top three strengths? What is my successful style? Combining these together, what are the specific things I can offer to a potential sponsor?' Let's explore some steps you can take along this road.

You can adopt the freelancer's approach

Tackle the exercise called *A Freelancer In Six Months*. Imagine that you were forced to go freelance in that time. What would you do? Don't worry about money for the moment. Describe:

a) the kind of work you would like to do
b) the services you would offer
c) the customers you would target
d) the benefits to these customers – what tangible rewards would they take away by buying your services?
e) the concrete steps you would take to get your first three customers.

Finally, clarify how you would develop what you offer into a brilliant niche service.

You can make what you offer 'of high value & hard to replace'

Take a look at *The Employability Model*. This plots your 'Value' to a sponsor against your 'Replaceability'. (Nobody is irreplaceable, but some are more replaceable than others.) Looking through the eyes of a potential employer, where do you fit on the model? Is your contribution:

● **Low Value/Easy To Replace**. For example, cleaners and Consultants. 'When in doubt, keep the cleaners,' some people advise managing directors. 'They are cheaper and get more visible results.' Joking aside, it is vital to move out of this quadrant, otherwise you become the modern equivalent of factory fodder. (continued on page 78)

The Employability Model

VALUE	**HIGH VALUE** **EASY TO REPLACE**	**HIGH VALUE** **HARD TO REPLACE**
	LOW VALUE **EASY TO REPLACE**	**LOW VALUE** **HARD TO REPLACE**

REPLACEABILITY

A FREELANCER
IN SIX MONTHS

If I had to go freelance in six months

The kind of work I would really like to do would be:

● _____

The products and services I would offer would be:

● _____

● _____

The kind of customers I would target would be:

● _____

The benefits these customers would get from purchasing these products and services would be:

● _____

● _____

The steps I would take to provide a brilliant niche service would be:

- _____

- _____

The steps I would take to get my first three customers would be:

- _____

- _____

The way I would charge for the products and services would be:

- _____

- _____

The other things I would do to build a successful business would be:

- _____

- _____

EMPLOYABILITY
My action plan

The place I rate myself now on the scale of value and replaceability is:

● _____

_____

The specific things I can do to make myself of high value and hard to replace are:

● _____

_____

● _____

_____

● _____

_____

- **High Value/Easy To Replace**. For example, marketing Departments. They are prime candidates for outsourcing. Sometimes they are great, sometimes they are obsessed by the latest marketing concepts, whether or not these fit the business strategy. If you outsource the marketing department, give them first crack at pitching for future assignments.

- **Low Value/Hard To Replace**. For example, departments that attempt to make themselves hard to replace by obscuring their work in the 'Black Arts'. IT, Finance and HR may soon be on this danger list.

- **High Value/Hard To Replace**. For example, brilliant niche providers who perform outstanding work, but are also willing to pass on their wisdom. Paradoxically, they make themselves valuable by giving away their knowledge, rather than by hoarding trade secrets.

Looking through the eyes of potential sponsors, where are you on The Employability Model? Where would you like to place yourself? How must you keep developing to stay in the top right hand corner, being of High Value and Hard To Replace?

You can transform your currency

How do you earn your living now? How would you like to earn your living in the future? Take a look at The Currency Curve. This plots your 'Currency', the way you earn your living, with your 'Career Development'. As people get older, they can find themselves reaching the top of the curve. At this point, they must embark on the next step in their professional development. Why? Otherwise they will be doing the same things in three years' time, but with less energy. Helen reinvented her job even before becoming a vet, but she must keep evolving. How can you transform your currency? Some key rules:

- **Build on your strengths, rather than focus on your weaknesses.** Who do you respect in your professional field? Ask them to define what you do best; then develop your top talents. Learn from leading-edge ideas in your field, adapt these in your own way and pilot these with customers. Build on what works and add it to your repertoire. Position what you offer in terms of specific customer benefits. Be a brilliant niche provider, rather than a generalist all rounder.

● **Provide the personal touch**.
Today people have masses of information at their finger tips which provides 'consciousness raising.' Individuals now want 'customisation.' They say: 'Yes, I understand the concept, but what about me? How can I apply it in my life and work?' Get to know each customer and, wherever possible, find concrete ways to help them to succeed.

● **Spend time with pacesetting customers. Work with them to develop your future products.**
Get alongside forward thinking customers. Look ahead to the challenges they face in the next few years. Share your know-how to help them tackle these issues successfully. Why? 'Today's customisation is tomorrow's commodity.' Spending time with leading-edge customers will develop the tools that other people will want tomorrow. You may even get your product development funded.

The currency curve

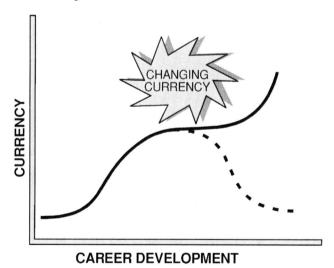

CHANGING CURRENCY

MY PRESENT CURRENCY
The way I earn my living now is:

- by _____

_____

- by _____

_____

- by _____

_____

MY FUTURE CURRENCY
The way I want to earn my living in the future is:

- by _____

_____

- by _____

_____

- by _____

_____

You can look for gaps in the market within your own company

'Personal circumstances dictate that I stay with my present employer,' explained Kathy, a middle manager. 'But my job is frustrating. How can I find my next career opportunity?' William Bridges tackles this quandary in his books, such as *Creating You & Co Inc*. He has developed an approach called 'Find-A-Need-And-Fill-It'. Looking at your present employer through the eyes of an entrepreneur, search for potential job opportunities. He invites you to answer the following questions.

- The challenges facing our company are …
- The future business opportunities are …
- The gaps in the wider market are …
- The pioneering products and services we can create are …
- The turnaround situations needed with clients are …
- The new and emerging problems in our company are …
- The internal roadblocks we face in our company are …
- The challenging interfaces between groups are …
- The missing pieces in our processes are …

How could you fill these gaps? Try tackling the exercise called *Find A Need And Fill It*. William Bridges suggests putting forward a proposal that will produce a 'Win-Win' for both you and the business. The key remains: 'Think like an entrepreneur, whether you work inside or outside a company.'

You can clarify your 'A' contribution to a business

'Good news and challenging news,' is the outlook when scanning the future world of work. First – the **Challenging News**. Successful employers will recruit, reward and retain 'A' players in each field. For example, they will hire people who are 'A' players as programmers, carpenters, educators, accountants, managers, leaders or other suppliers. They will try to avoid hiring 'B' players or 'C' players. Second, the **Good News**. Everybody is an 'A' player at something. Try tackling the exercise called *My 'A' Contribution To A Business*. Being completely honest, describe:

    a)   the activities where I consistently deliver As are ...
    b)   the activities where I consistently deliver Bs are ...
    c)   the activities where I consistently deliver Cs are ...

Jim Collins, author of *Built To Last*, has studied what outstanding leaders do to move teams from 'being good to great.' One key factor: 'They get the right people on the bus; the wrong people off the bus; and the right people in the right places on the bus.' What is your best place on the bus? The future is bright, providing you keep developing as an 'A' Player.

You can clarify what, for you, would be a fulfilling role

John, a pioneer by nature, felt stuck. During his 20s, he founded and sold a computer business. Wooed by a market leader who offered him full-time employment, he spent his 30s travelling the world, building businesses in fresh territories. Reaching his 40s, the company recalled him to HQ, charged with executing strategies previously decided by 'committees.' Adrenalin-driven, John felt like an undercover cop retired to a desk job. Taking a blank sheet of paper, he headed it *My Fulfilling Role*. Beginning by looking at his own drivers, he listed the characteristics he wanted in a job.

These were: shaping strategy ... creating 'prototypes' that prove profitable ... working with stimulating people in uncharted territory ... stretching myself to deliver ... developing products that improve peoples' lives.

John fashioned a role based on these qualities. Looking around the company, he pulled together three existing projects to start a new venture. The aim – to create software that enabled students to take more charge of their learning. How to get funding? Governments disillusioned with the academic world offered to trial the product. John is now in the process of ensuring the software becomes another 'Profitable Prototype'.

How to create a fulfilling role? If you wish, try adopting this 'inside out' approach to inventing a job. First, start by clarifying your own motivators. Second, bearing these drivers in mind, craft a role that benefits both yourself and your employers. Become part of the movement towards creating 'new' jobs. Years ago, people relied on getting promotion into a suitable 'box', which came complete with an age-old job description. If the role proved unsatisfying, however, the employee waited for the next re-organisation. Today, people recognise that millions of future jobs have not yet been invented. Perhaps you can create one by tackling the exercise called *My Fulfilling Role*.

You can clarify your special contribution

What can you offer to a sponsor? Let's reflect on the questions we have covered so far. If you were a Managing Director, what would you hire yourself to deliver? How can you make this 'High Value and Hard To Replace'? Where are you now on the Currency Curve? How do you want to earn your living in the future? How can you get alongside pacesetters and create your new products? What are the activities where you consistently deliver A's?' Try tackling the exercise called *My Special Contribution*. Clarify the three things you can offer an employer. Bearing in mind that people buy benefits, how will your contribution help them to achieve success?

Time to move on to the next step. So far we have considered your vocation. Let's explore how to choose the right vehicles, which also involves finding people who will pay you for performing valuable work.

FIND A NEED AND FILL IT

Proactive people continually scan the business for possible ways to make their future contribution. Here are some questions they use for exploring what might be possible. They are based on William Bridges 'Find-A-Need-And-Fill-It' Career Option Grid. You can use them for crafting your next contribution to the company.

The challenges facing the company are:

● _____

The specific things I could offer in these areas are:

● _____

The future business opportunities are:

● _____

The specific things I could offer in these areas are:

● _____

The gaps in the market are:

● _____

The specific things I could offer in these areas are:

● _____

The pioneering products and services we can create are:

● _____

The specific things I could offer in these areas are:

● _____

The turnaround situations needed with clients are:

● _____

The specific things I could offer in these areas are:

● _____

The turnaround situations
needed in our company are:

● _____

The new and emerging
problems are:

● _____

The internal roadblocks we
face in our company are:

● _____

The challenging interfaces
between groups are:

● _____

The missing pieces
in our processes are:

● _____

The other things we must
do to be successful are:

● _____

The specific things I could
offer in these areas are:

● _____

The specific things I could
offer in these areas are:

● _____

The specific things I could
offer in these areas are:

● _____

The specific things I could
offer in these areas are:

● _____

The specific things I could
offer in these areas are:

● _____

The specific things I could
offer in these areas are:

● _____

MY 'A' CONTRIBUTION
TO A BUSINESS

'A's - the activities where I consistently deliver 'A's are when I am:

- _____   - _____

- _____   - _____

'B's - the activities where I consistently deliver 'B's are when I am:

- _____   - _____

'C's - the activities where I consistently deliver 'C's are when I am:

- _____   - _____

My 'A' contribution - bearing this in mind, I believe my best contribution to an employer would be:

- to _____

- to _____

- to _____

MY FULFILLING ROLE

The characteristics and qualities I want in a role to make it fulfilling for me are that it should be one where I am able:

- to _____

- to _____

- to _____

- to _____

- to _____

The specific things I can do to find or create this kind of role are:

- I can _____

- I can _____

- I can _____

MY SPECIAL CONTRIBUTION

The special contribution I can make to a potential sponsor is:

- I can _____

- I can _____

- I can _____

The benefits that this contribution can deliver to a potential sponsor are:

- _____

- _____

- _____

- _____

STEP TWO
VEHICLES
Following Your Vocation

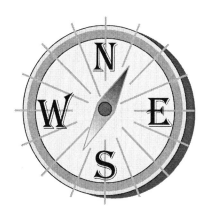

THE
MAGIC
OF
WORK

*How you can balance your
Soul Work and Salary Work*

Introduction

How to balance your mission and mortgage? Rewarding work is okay; but who pays the rent? Start from the big picture and find an enriching way to employ your talents. Your vocation may remain constant but, over the years, you will express it via different vehicles. Imagine that your life-theme is 'Creating beauty.' You can be a painter, musician, architect, chef, interior designer, landscape gardener, environmentalist or whatever. During the early part of your life in particular, you will experiment with many ways of translating your theme into action.

How to find the right vehicle? As we mentioned at the start of the book, two guidelines are worth considering.

1. Choose a '**Field**' of work you find fascinating. Select one where you feel at ease and yet also excel. For example, you may feel 'at home' working with technology, business, science, sport, the arts, people-management or whatever.
2. Choose the '**Form**' of work that fits your personality. For example, you may prefer to work as an individual, be a team member, run a business or whatever.

Try tackling the exercise called *My Vehicles*. First, describe your vocation. Second, describe the possible vehicles you can use for expressing this vocation. Third, describe the value that you will provide to potential buyers.

'But how do you get money?' you may ask. 'I hate promoting myself.' Reach out to customers in the way you find natural. Sounds idealistic. How to put this principle into practice? The following pages consider steps you can take to find *Sponsors*, set *Specific Goals*, do *Superb Work get Support*. Let's explore how to fund your labour of love.

MY VEHICLES

VOCATION
I believe my vocation is:

- to _____

_____

VEHICLES
The different vehicles I can use to express my vocation are:

- I can _____

- I can _____

- I can _____

VALUE
The value I can offer to potential sponsors is that I can help them:

- to _____

- to _____

- to _____

Sponsors

Looking for your next role? Good news and bad news. Starting with the latter, old-style methods of job search resemble a lottery and can destroy your self-confidence. Don't rely on applying for jobs that are advertised, because around 250 other candidates are vying for that position. CVs seldom show your full abilities and may not even get you past the gatekeeper. Recruitment agencies can be okay, but don't expect personal attention. Pressurised to hit targets, they may be tempted to find you a job where they quickly bag their commission. Retain old-style methods as part of your repertoire, but see anything you get as a bonus.

What is the good news? People buy people. Employers are looking for certainty in an increasingly uncertain world. They want cast-iron guarantees, so are likely to hire somebody who has a track record of delivering results. Your next role is likely to come through somebody you know already. Alternatively, it may be via a benefactor who recommends you to a decision-maker. 'But I am hopeless at keeping in touch with people,' you may say. 'I prefer to keep a low profile.' Start by maintaining contact with kindred spirits.

You can make a map of your network

Think like a freelancer. Imagine that you must generate your own business. Exercise your entrepreneurial muscle, especially if you work full-time in a company. Rule 1: Build from a position of strength. Make a brilliant contribution to the business and build a reputation for finishing. Sponsors who say: 'That person delivers the goods,' are your best advert. Rule 2: Shape your own destiny, rather than leave it in the hands of others. Take initiatives, rather than become institutionalised.

Tackle the exercise called *My Network*. Draw a map showing the names of all the people you know. Who are your vocational soul mates? Who might be potential sponsors inside your present company? Who are the people who have moved on to fresh fields?

Who have become decision makers? At this point, don't worry if they do not have a budget. 'But I only know a few people,' is a common response. Think for a while. Who have you had contact with in the past 10 years? Go deeper and deeper. It's guaranteed that you will have many more contacts that you initially believed. Continue drawing until you have at least 20 names on the map of your network.

You can follow your natural way of networking

Keep in touch with people in a way that fits your values-system. Many people feel uneasy 'selling' or imposing themselves on potential employers. Good networkers maintain contact by adopting methods they find natural. One approach is to: 'Be a giver, rather than a grabber.' Share knowledge, ideas and tools that will help people to be successful. (This is often the best method if you plan to continue working in your present company.) Remember, it may take up to a year of investing time in potential sponsors before the right opportunity appears. Tackle the exercise called *My Natural Way of Networking*. Here are some suggestions you may want to consider:

a) Maintain contact with people through e-mail, For example, by sharing know-how, articles, books, etc. that may help them to tackle their challenges successfully.
b) Meet up with potential sponsors. For example, to simply catch-up with them, to share success stories, or to do some creative problem solving on an issue they face in their business.

MY NETWORK

Personal recommendation is the best advertisement and people often buy through networks. How big is your network? Who do you know who might buy your products or services? Who do you know who has contacts? Draw a map of your personal network. Start with the people you know best, plus any customers, then expand your map. List everybody who might buy your products or put you in touch with potential customers.

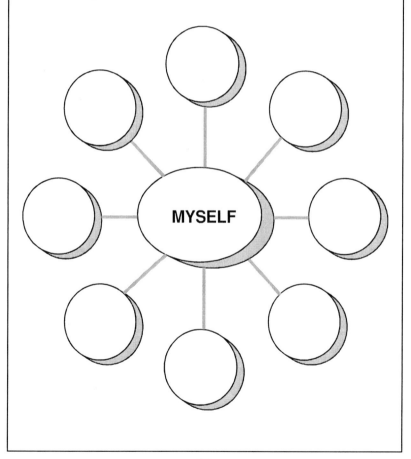

MY NATURAL WAY
OF WORKING

The natural ways for me to keep in touch with my
network would be:

- to _____

- to _____

- to _____

The specific steps I can take to maintain contact with my
network are:

- to _____

- to _____

- to _____

One rule above all – help the people in your network to succeed. Be sensible, of course – do not become a victim or a suffering martyr. Some people will respond in kind, others will drain energy without giving in return. Build with those who treat you fairly.

You can clarify the challenges facing potential sponsors

Put on your business hat. Start by looking at your present workplace. Who are the potential sponsors? For example, the Managing Director; your manager; other key people. Looking at your wider network, who are other potential sponsors? Who can make decisions about their budget? Who might be able to find some kind of funding? Look at the world from their perspective. Considering each potential sponsor in turn, ask yourself:

- What burning issues are keeping them awake at night?
- What challenges are their businesses facing?
- What challenges are they personally facing?
- What results do they want delivered?
- What is happening in their market?
- What must their businesses do to stay ahead of the field?
- What can I offer to help them to achieve success?

Tackle the exercise called *Potential Sponsors: The Challenges They Face*. Whether you aim to work within your present company or search elsewhere, consider how to help the potential buyers to achieve their goals.

You can clarify how to 'position' what you offer

'Positioning is all,' we are told. How can you present what you offer in a way customers find attractive? Show how it will help them in their daily work. As we are frequently told: 'People buy benefits, not features.' Bear two things in mind when tackling the exercise on this theme. First, your aim is to help the sponsor to succeed. Second, you are 'selling results'; you are not selling yourself. Positioning also involves reaching kindred spirits, the people with whom you work best. Who are you favourite customers? What are their personality characteristics? 'But shouldn't I take every possible job?' you may ask. Bills must be paid, so you will start out by grasping every opportunity. As the years roll by, however, your professional passion may fluctuate. While you still do a good job with most clients, working with certain customers is a real pleasure. Can you create more opportunities to generate such positive energy? Try tackling the exercise called *My Perfect Customer*.

You can target rising businesses, rather than dying businesses

'Bankruptcy was just around the corner two years ago,' reported one manufacturer. 'My problem was that I got caught in a comfortable, long-term contract supplying services to the car industry. The downturn came and it took 18 months to recover. Never again will I be beholden to a company that is on its last legs.'

What is the source of your income? Does it spring from yesterday's, today's or tomorrow's businesses? Where will the money come from in the future? Old-style firms are more likely to concentrate on cost cutting as they attempt to squeeze the last drop from redundant business models. New-style firms are more likely to expand, have money and be open to fresh ideas. Try tackling the exercise on this theme. First, describe what you see as Rising Businesses. Second, describe the people you know who work in these companies. Third, describe the steps you can take to get in touch with these people. Targeting tomorrow's companies can lay the foundations for future success.

You can be ready for when somebody says: 'How can we take this further?'

Be prepared to act quickly when somebody offers you business. For example, fifteen years ago, I earned my living running workshops on Leadership. While looking to do one-to-one work, I had reframed visits to potential sponsors as opportunities to share ideas about Mentoring. Then one day a Managing Director said: 'How can we take this further? I would like to implement mentoring across the company. Can I have a proposal within 48 hours?' The laptop hummed in the hotel room that night.

Prospecting can be tiring, especially if it proves fruitless, so what to do after striking gold? First, respond with a proposal and, if possible, make a contract with the sponsor. Second, redouble your efforts. Months of mining have finally paid off and you have hit a rich seam. The last thing to do is knock-off for lunch. (Or extend your overdraft, buying the latest office furniture.) Reach out to your network and fill your schedule. Sponsors are likely to hire suppliers with busy diaries, rather than those with a begging bowl. Don't worry if you fill your timetable; you can then concentrate on the customers with whom you work best.

'But what about money?' you may ask. 'I feel uncomfortable asking for payment.' Be prepared to invest a lot of free time up-front. When you feel it is appropriate, however, raise the issue of payment. Some superb sales people never mention 'money'. They talk about 'investment' or use phrases like: 'Is it possible to get any funding?' This approach can be surprisingly successful.

Time to move onto the next stage. Imagine that you have been accepted for a role, found a project or been hired to deliver tangible results. Let's explore how to make clear contracts with your *Sponsors.*

POTENTIAL SPONSORS:
The challenges they face

The potential sponsor's name is:

● _____

The challenges they face are:

● _____

● _____

● _____

The results they may want delivered are:

● _____

● _____

● _____

The specific things I could offer to help them to achieve these results are:

● _____

● _____

● _____

POSITIONING

The specific results I can deliver to a potential employer are:

- _____

- _____

- _____

The potential employers who might be interested in these results are:

- _____

- _____

- _____

The things I can do to position what I offer in a way that is attractive and will help them achieve success are:

- _____

- _____

- _____

MY PERFECT CUSTOMER

My perfect customer would be somebody who:

- _____

- _____

- _____

The specific things I can do to reach this kind of customer are:

- _____

- _____

- _____

The specific things I can offer to this kind of customer are:

- _____

- _____

- _____

RISING BUSINESSES

The rising businesses are:

- _____
- _____
- _____

The people I know who work in these rising businesses are:

- _____   - _____
- _____   - _____
- _____   - _____

The specific steps I can take to reach these people are:

- _____
- _____
- _____

Specific Goals

'Keep focusing on the picture of perfection,' is good advice. Satisfying sponsors is crucial, but so is satisfying the soul. Take time out to get an overview and see things in perspective. Check with your internal compass by reflecting back on exercises such as *Success* and *My Legacy*. Make sure that taking the next step will help you to travel towards your goals.

'My first contract is with myself; then it is easier to make contracts with other people,' explained one person. Why? Otherwise it is easy to have a meeting and be persuaded into following somebody else's agenda. Commercial arrangements may call for making detours, of course, so try to find mutual win-wins. This involves a two-stage process. First, contract with yourself on your specific goals. Second, contract with sponsors on their specific goals. Let's explore how to make this happen.

You can take responsibility for working towards your specific goals

Get in the helicopter. Take an overview of your options before making agreements with a sponsor. For example, imagine that you work in a company and have occupied your present role for the past 12 months. Corporate reorganisation time has arrived and you have been invited to lead a new business team. Try tackling the exercise called *My Future Work*. Make a map of the possible roads you can follow in the future. For instance:

a) stay in my present role
b) take the leadership role
c) craft my perfect role inside the company
d) become an outside supplier to my present company
e) move to a competitor
f) do something completely different.

Bearing in mind your deepest drivers, consider each route and describe the pluses and minuses. Rate how attractive each route is to you. Do this on a scale 0-10. Employing your imagination, look for any possible combinations from each option. Then make a new road from these possibilities in the exercise called *My Chosen Road*.

If you have been invited to lead the new business team, how does the role fit with your long-term life goals? You may see taking the assignment as:

- **a fully satisfying step** – it will be fulfilling and carry you along your chosen road
- **a semi-satisfying step** – perhaps you can re-craft the role to make it more exciting
- **a not-so satisfying step** – perhaps it is possible to reframe the role, seeing it as contributing to your longer-term goals
- **a holding-position** – performing it will buy you time to do parallel work on pursuing your chosen road
- **a detour** – taking the job will move you away from your drivers, thus leading to dissatisfaction.

MY FUTURE WORK

This exercise is in several parts.

First, make a map of the possible roads you can take in your future work. Second, describe the pluses and minuses of each option. Third, rate how attractive each of these options is to you. Do this on a scale 0-10. Finally, be creative and look for any possible combinations from each option. Then make a new road from these possibilities in the next exercise called *My Chosen Road*.

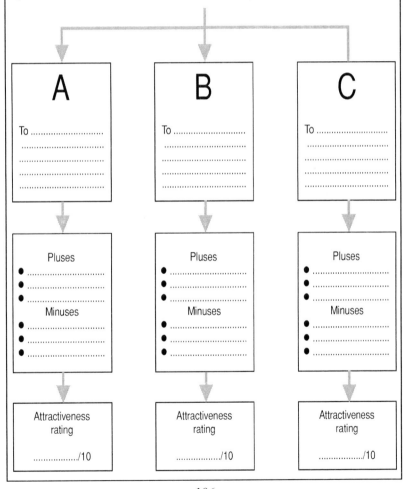

A

To ....
....
....
....
....

Pluses
- ....
- ....
- ....

Minuses
- ....
- ....
- ....

Attractiveness rating

................/10

B

To ....
....
....
....
....

Pluses
- ....
- ....
- ....

Minuses
- ....
- ....
- ....

Attractiveness rating

................/10

C

To ....
....
....
....
....

Pluses
- ....
- ....
- ....

Minuses
- ....
- ....
- ....

Attractiveness rating

................/10

MY CHOSEN ROAD

Now onto the creative part. First, take a look at the different roads you can follow. Which is your preferred road? How can you put together a new road that includes the best parts of each road? Second, complete the exercise by drawing the road that you want to take. If you are about to take a new role or project, how does this fit with following your chosen road in the future?

My chosen road is:

- to _____

- to _____

- to _____

My Action Plan for following this road is:

- to _____

- to _____

- to _____

Looking at your possible route forward, it's time to make a conscious decision. Bearing in mind the whole package, complete with pluses and minuses, do you want to take the assignment? Does it fit with your long-term goals? Does it need reframing? For example, a budding actor may see their part-time job waiting on tables as necessary for financing early morning auditions. Be careful if you opt for reframing. Sometimes it can be real; sometimes it can be a delusion.

Let's imagine you decide to take an assignment, be it a new role in your company, providing services as an outside supplier or whatever. The next step is making clear contracts with your employer, which calls for managing upwards. Sometimes this is simple; sometimes it can be complicated.

You can take responsibility for setting specific goals with your sponsor

Clear contracting is vital in any relationship. This is especially so when providing products or services to a sponsor. At the end of the contracting process, it is important to make sure that everybody is agreed upon:

a) *what* mountain you are climbing – the specific results to be delivered

b) *why* you are climbing it – the benefits to the business

c) *how* you can to climb it – the rules to follow and the freedom you will have to do things your own way

d) *what* resources you will need – the support required to complete the job

e) *when* you will reach the summit – the specific dates when results must be delivered.

Sounds simple in theory, what about the practice? Let's consider how contracting can lay the foundations for a good working relationship.

You can prepare properly before the contracting meeting with the sponsor

Dave, a successful soccer manager, had the chance to take a step forward in his career. Three leading clubs had offered him interviews for the vacant post of manager. Performing excellent work in the past had placed him in the position where he had options, but now the contracting process would be crucial. Playing the scenarios in his mind, Dave rehearsed his plan for each of the interviews. He needed to:

- be warm, friendly and demonstrate his football knowledge, thus confirming his reputation for having people-management skills and technical coaching ability

- show respect to the employers, but also ensure he covered his agenda in the meeting

- show his belief in the club, but also show the Directors that he understood the issues they were facing, such as the financial and playing challenges confronting the club

- clarify the Directors' goals for the club, such as the results they wanted delivered both on and off the field – he must then 'play back' the goals to show he understood their ambitions

- share his goals for the team and reassure the Directors that he would get some early successes towards achieving their targets for the club

- indicate he was extremely interested in the management position – he would quickly get back to the Directors with a concrete proposal on how to achieve the club's goals

- explain his approach to the job – he would ask if it was okay to be honest; to describe his way of working; and also outline the resources required to achieve the goals.

Dave wanted to cover the following points. First, he looked forward to the possibility of managing the club, but also had two other offers to explore. Second, if the Directors wanted him to become manager, he would need certain resources. Dave would appoint his own management team; require a substantial transfer budget, etc. Third, he had certain management beliefs. During the first months, 'established' players might challenge his authority. At this point, he would make his 'rules' clear; the players must decide whether or not to opt-in. (He would have already lined up better replacements for those players who chose to move on.)

● conclude the meeting in a positive way.

Dave planned to reassure the Directors he would deliver their goals for the club. He would put together a proposal for taking the team forward, getting it back to them within 48 hours. The proposal would highlight some 'early wins' that could be achieved to raise the fans' confidence, thus improving season ticket sales. The Directors would obviously then decide whether or not they wanted him to become manager.

Writing his script for each interview, Dave felt the crucial parts were agreeing on the goals, plus obtaining the support required to do the job. Two clubs might not accede to his 'rules' for getting the results. Why? First, they both owed money to the bank after recent ground expansion, thus reducing available transfer funds. Second, they might balk at him appointing his own management team. Nevertheless, he decided to give each interview his best shot. (Dave was offered all three posts. He opted for the club where the Directors did not prevaricate; they enthusiastically provided the resources on the spot.)

Back to your assignment. Mentally rehearse your meeting with the sponsor. What are the challenges they face? What will be their picture of perfection? What is their management style – do they focus on people, products or profitability? Do they like people to talk about the big vision or prefer nitty-gritty details? Maybe you will have multiple sponsors. If so, research each person and discover their goals. Consider how to manage any conflicts. What resources are required to do the job? How can you deliver early guaranteed successes? Let's explore some of these steps.

You can anticipate the sponsor's view of the specific goals

Perhaps you have already agreed your targets. If not, look at the world from their point of view. Start by tackling two exercises on this theme. First – *Standing In The Sponsor's Shoes*. Ask yourself: 'If I was in their position, what results would I ask me to deliver?' Be extremely demanding. Second – *Success: The Actual Words People Will Be Saying*. List the key people you must satisfy. For example: MD; sponsor; department heads; customers and team members. Pick a date in the future, such as in 12 months. Write the 'Actual Words' you want people to be saying at that time. You may want your sponsor to say: 'I can rely on this person entirely. They always fulfil promises. The customers are giving stunning feedback.' Clarify your strategies for ensuring they say these things in one year.

STANDING IN THE SPONSOR'S SHOES

If I were in my sponsor's shoes, the results I would ask me to deliver would be:

1. **to** _____

    The specific things that would be happening that would tell me I have reached this goal would be:

    ● _____

    ● _____

    ● _____

2. **to** _____

    The specific things that would be happening that would tell me I have reached this goal would be:

    ● _____

    ● _____

    ● _____

3. **to** _____

    The specific things that would be happening that would tell me I have reached this goal would be:

    ● _____

    ● _____

    ● _____

SUCCESS

The actual words people will be saying

List all the key people you must satisfy. Pick a date in the future. Describe the 'actual words' you want these people to be saying at that time. Then determine how to do your best to ensure they are saying these things. (Note: While the exercise says 'Person', you can list specific target groups. Bear in mind, however, that there may be people with different needs within these groups.)

The date _____

Person A _____

The actual words I want them to be saying are:

' _____ ,

' _____ ,

' _____ ,

Person B _____

' _____ ,

' _____ ,

' _____ ,

Person C _____

' _____ '

' _____ '

' _____ '

Person D _____

' _____ '

' _____ '

' _____ '

Person E _____

' _____ '

' _____ '

' _____ '

The specific things I can do to do my best to ensure they are saying these things are:

● I can _____

● I can _____

● I can _____

You can clarify the pluses and minuses involved in achieving the goals

Dave recognised both the rewards and risks involved in taking the manager's position. The positives: an exciting job at a go-ahead club; great backing from the Chairman; the chance to take the team into Europe. The negatives: perhaps initial battles with disgruntled players who had previously ruled the dressing room. Dave believed athletes must take care of their bodies, rather than refuel with alcohol, but this might meet resistance. He reframed such conflicts as an opportunity. Players who refused to sign-up to the new rules would be transferred. One further 'risk' – he was putting his reputation on the line. Dave lived in the realm of possibilities rather than problems, however; so going beyond his comfort zone offered the chance to improve both himself and the club.

Time to look at your new role. What will be the upsides and downsides? Try tackling the exercise called *Achieving The Goals: The Pluses And Minuses*. Describe the positives and negatives: a) for the business; b) for the sponsors; c) for the customers; d) for any other groups; e) for yourself. How can you maximise the pluses? How can you minimise the minuses? Pay special attention to any possible negative consequences for key stakeholders in the business, such as your project cutting across their agendas. If necessary, spend time with such people to work out win-wins, otherwise they may sabotage your efforts. Bearing in mind all these pluses and minuses, are you prepared to accept the whole package?

You can rate your motivation and your chances of success

Looking at the mountain to climb, does the challenge put a spring into your step? Try tackling exercise called *My Motivation For Achieving The Goals*. Rate the attractiveness on a scale 0-10. Scoring 7+ is a promising start. Scoring less than 7 is a danger signal, so think twice before scaling the glacier. Move on to the exercise called *Rating The*

Chances Of Success. Looking at the whole picture, calculate the chances of delivering the goals. The same rules apply. Scoring 7+ is okay, but find specific ways to boost this figure, otherwise you may get into the job and find that your hands are tied. Remember – there are two occasions when you have the greatest leverage. First, before you take the role. Second, early on when you deliver some early wins. Give yourself a fighting chance by capitalising on these opportunities and getting the resources required to reach the summit.

You can clarify ways to reassure your sponsor

One thing is guaranteed, sponsors will continually test your reliability. 'But I want them to trust me,' you may say. Forget it. As one MD put it: 'I believe in certainty, not trust. When the Red Arrows turn right, they know everybody has turned right.' During the early days you will still be on trial. Sponsors will visit your part of the business and 'jump on the floor boards' to see if they are shaky. Ensure they don't find problems; otherwise they will meddle and make your life a misery.

Plan how to keep the sponsors off your back. Two suggestions. First, reassure them you will deliver results. Get an early success, keep all your promises and show you will meet the long-term targets. Second, reassure them you see the potential problems they may be registering on their 'Radar'. Leaders often worry that others fail to spot warning signs, so demonstrate they you can anticipate and prevent difficulties. Putting their mind at rest will buy time to get on with the real work. Try tackling the exercise on this theme called *Reassuring The Sponsor*.

You can meet with your sponsor to agree on the picture of perfection

Decision makers are busy people, so be proactive in setting up the final contracting meeting. While not wanting to clutter their diary, you do need airtime together. Set a date and flag up the agenda. Be business-like during the meeting. Clarify the sponsor's picture of perfection. Play it back to ensure you agree on the 'What'. Move onto the 'How'. Make sure you have the necessary autonomy and required support. Reassure them you recognise potential problems that may be on their 'Radar'. Ask how they want to be kept up-to-date. Conclude by making clear contracts. Emerging from the meeting, you should have crystal-clear agreements about:

- the **what** – the specific results to delivered
- the **how** – the autonomy you will have and the support that will be given
- the **when** – the delivery dates and how your sponsor wants to be kept informed.

What if the meeting produces confusion? The relationship may be disastrous; the goal posts may shift; the support may not be forthcoming. Don't be afraid to ask for time to reflect. Explain that you will respond with a proposal. If you decide to take the role, describe the results you will deliver. (You may wish to follow the framework outlined in the exercise *My Agreed Goals*.) What if you decide to say 'No, thanks'? Engineer a positive exit. Always try to be diplomatic, because you may bump into these potential sponsors in the future. If you commit yourself to reaching the targets, however, you will move onto the next stage. Let's consider how to perform *Superb Work*.

ACHIEVING THE GOALS:
The pluses and the minuses

Describe what you see as the pluses and minuses of achieving the goals:

FOR:	PLUSES	MINUSES
The business	• _____	• _____
	• _____	• _____
The sponsors	• _____	• _____
	• _____	• _____
The customers	• _____	• _____
	• _____	• _____
Any other groups	• _____	• _____
	• _____	• _____
Myself	• _____	• _____
	• _____	• _____

MY MOTIVATION FOR ACHIEVING THE GOALS

The goals are:

- to _____

- to _____

- to _____

PLUSES
The pluses of reaching the goals will be:

- _____   - _____

- _____   - _____

- _____   - _____

MINUSES
The minuses of reaching the goals will be:

- _____   - _____

- _____   - _____

- _____   - _____

My motivation rating for reaching the goals is:

_____/**10**

RATING THE CHANCES OF SUCCESS

My present assessment of the chances of delivering success is:

_____/10

The specific things that would need to be done to increase the chances of success are:

- to _____
- to _____
- to _____

The specific things I can do before taking the role, in order to ensure the greatest chance of success, are:

- to _____
- to _____
- to _____

REASSURING THE SPONSOR

RESULTS
The specific things I can do to reassure my sponsor that
I have a crystal-clear picture of the results to be
delivered are:

- to _____

- to _____

- to _____

RADAR
The specific things I can do to reassure my sponsor that
I understand the concerns that might be on their radar
are:

- to _____

- to _____

- to _____

REASSURANCE
The other things that I can do to reassure my sponsor
that I will deliver the results are:

- to _____

- to _____

- to _____

MY AGREED GOALS

My specific goals are:

1. to _____

Sub-goals

- to _____

- to _____

- to _____

2. to _____

Sub-goals

- to _____

- to _____

- to _____

3. to _____

Sub-goals

- to _____

- to _____

- to _____

Superb Work

Great work beckons – how can you deliver the goods? Start by learning from your own experience. Look back at your life and tackle the exercise called *My Superb Work*. Describe a time when you performed brilliantly. Perhaps you were working alone; perhaps you were working in a team. What did you do right to stretch yourself and achieve success? How can you apply these principles to your latest project and produce great work? Time to move onto learning from other people.

'They are a Class Act,' is a phrase used to describe somebody who consistently performs brilliantly. For example, Pele in soccer, Kiri Te Kanawa in music, Raymond Blanc in food and The Dalai Lama in spiritual matters. Try tackling the exercise on this theme. Write the name of somebody who you believe is a Class Act. Describe what they do right and how you can follow these principles in your work. Great performers often demonstrate five qualities. They focus on **Character, Competence, Consistency, Creativity** and **Class**. Let's explore how you can take these steps by moving onto the exercise called *Becoming A Class Act*.

CHARACTER: You can build on the strengths in your character

Great performers have the right character for the job. On a scale 0-10, to what extent do you believe you have the right personality for your work? The key is to make sure you are in your element. Tom Peters has the charisma to captivate large audiences; other people feel more comfortable doing one-to-one sessions. Assuming you feel 'at home' in your profession, how can you continue to develop the right attitude to succeed in your chosen field? Here are some suggestions.

MY SUPERB WORK

(a) Describe a time when you did some superb work. It could have been work you did by yourself or with other people.

● When I _____

(b) Describe what you did right then to do superb work. Be as specific as possible.

● I _____

● I _____

● I _____

● I _____

● I _____

(c) How can you follow these principles again in the future? Describe the steps you can take to do superb work. If you wish, apply these to your latest project.

● I can _____

● I can _____

● I can _____

A Class Act

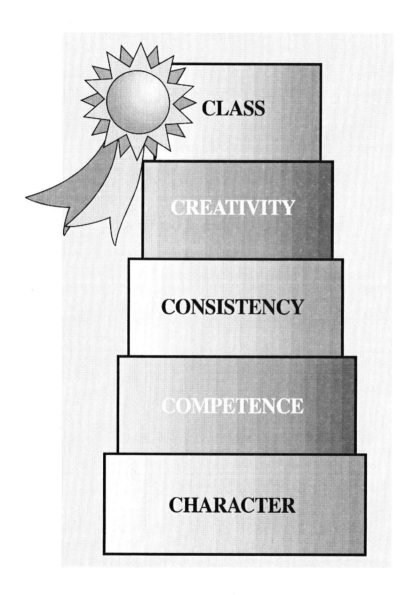

A CLASS ACT

(a) Write the name of a person who you believe is, or has been, 'a class act'.

● _____

(b) Write five things you believe he or she did right to be a class act

● _____

● _____

● _____

● _____

● _____

(c) How can you follow these paths in your own way? Describe three steps you can take in your own work to be a class act.

● I can _____

● I can _____

● I can _____

BECOMING A CLASS ACT (1)

'They are a class act,' is a phrase sometimes used to describe a performance in sports, the arts or other fields of work. How do you rate your performance in your chosen field? On a scale 0-10, rate yourself in the following areas.

● CHARACTER

Rate yourself on having the right attitude and character to succeed in your chosen field

● COMPETENCE

Rate yourself on having the skills and competence to succeed in your chosen field

● CONSISTENCY

Rate yourself on having the right consistency of performance to succeed in your chosen field

● CREATIVITY

Rate yourself on having the creativity to succeed in your chosen field

● CLASS

Rate yourself on having that extra touch of class that will make you outstanding in your chosen field

Start by following your successful patterns. How does this work in practice? Try tackling the exercise called *Building On My Preferred Working Style*. Take an honest look at yourself and your delivery targets. Bearing in mind your track record, go through the following steps. First, describe the things you do like to do in your work. Decide how to capitalise on these activities in your new role. Second, describe the things you don't like to do in your work. Decide how to compensate for, or manage, these activities in your new role. Third, describe your action plan for following your preferred working style. Then work hard to deliver the required results.

What about the gaps in your repertoire? Surround yourself with a Super Team. Great teams are made up of people who have 'Similarity Of Spirit and Diversity Of Strengths.' Gather together people who share similar values, but who have complementary skills. Get the right balance of 'Soul Players' and 'Star Players'. Co-ordinate their collective strengths to complete the tasks. Make sure you have the character – and the characters – to be successful in your chosen field. Time to look at the next quality exhibited by people who perform brilliantly.

COMPETENCE: You can make sure you demonstrate the right competence

Great workers have the competence to do the job. How do you rate your own ability in your chosen field? On a scale 0-10, to what extent do you have the talent and skills to reach your goals? If you have got what it takes, the next step is to translate this potential into daily actions. How to make this happen? Athletes tell us the Golden Rule is to 'Focus'. Concentrate on the key strategies that will give you the greatest chance of achieving success. Tackle the exercise called *Successful Strategies*. Look at your specific goals, then complete the following sentence (see continuation on page 131):

BUILDING ON MY PREFERRED WORKING STYLE

The things I like to do in work are:

- to _____
- to _____
- to _____
- to _____
- to _____

The specific ways I can do more of these things in my work are:

- to _____
- to _____
- to _____
- to _____
- to _____

The things I don't like to do in my work are:

- to _____

- to _____

- to _____

The ways I can compensate for, or find other ways to manage, these things are:

- to _____

- to _____

- to _____

My plan for building on my preferred working style and delivering the required results is:

- to _____

- to _____

- to _____

The three key things I can do to give myself the greatest chance of success are:

1) to _____

2) to _____

3) to _____

Peak performers dream, do and deliver. Translate your top line strategies into specific tasks; then complete these in your daily work. Whether you are a surgeon, pilot, athlete or whatever, the first step is to demonstrate professional competence. Getting the basics right provides certainty for our sponsors and the springboard for making full use of our talents.

CONSISTENCY: You can continually deliver consistency

Great performers score at least 8/10 on always producing top quality work. Excellent chefs, singers and athletes, for example, feel gutted if they fall from their high standards. On a scale 0-10, how do you rate yourself on consistently doing fine work? 'I can always count on you,' is a compliment from sponsors. Thunderbolts might be crashing around your ears, but people can still rely on your contribution. But what if you depend on other team members?

Great soccer teams, for example, often have three kinds of players. They have Commanding Players, Consistent Players and Creative Players. Commanding Players take charge on the field, Consistent Players always reach a certain standard. During a 38-match season, they will play well in at least 30 games. They do the right things in the right way every day to produce the right results. Consistent Players are the heart and soul of the team. Creative Players add the extra magic.

SUCCESSFUL STRATEGIES

The three things that I can do to give myself the greatest chance of success are:

1. to _____

   _____

   _____

2. to _____

   _____

   _____

3. to _____

   _____

   _____

SUCCESS:
Making it happen

THE **FIRST** STRATEGY IS:

● to _____

_____

The specific things I can do to make this happen are:

● _____

● _____

● _____

● _____

● _____

● _____

THE **SECOND** STRATEGY IS:

- to _____

_____

The specific things I can do to make this happen are:

- _____

- _____

- _____

THE **THIRD** STRATEGY IS:

- to _____

_____

The specific things I can do to make this happen are:

- _____

- _____

- _____

'But I'm a bit of each kind of player,' you may argue. Certainly this will be the case when pursuing your labour of love. Then you will take command, perform consistent work and add that touch of creativity. Great teams often have people who score highly in all three categories – but what if this isn't possible in your team? Get the right mix of people. Consistent Players will provide the foundation; then add others who produce that piece of magic. This leads us to the next step.

CREATIVITY: You can employ your creativity

Great workers are hungry to find fresh ways of improving their performance. On a scale 0-10, rate yourself on having the creativity to succeed in your chosen field. One key point – Class Acts get the right balance between continuity and change. Placido Domingo loves music and football, but sticks to singing and conducting. He does not juggle a ball on stage for three hours. Customers want to purchase a predictable experience. When undergoing a brain operation, you would prefer the surgeons to use their imagination within strict guidelines. Try tackling the exercise called *Continuity and Creativity*. Describe the areas of your work where: (a) you can provide certainty, (b) you can provide fresh approaches.

'But don't we really need Quantum Leap Thinking?' you may ask. That depends on to what extent you want to stay within the confines of your present business. Pacesetters produce fresh ideas that make the new rules for the game. For example, they introduce the Walkman; Telephone Banking or Low Cost Airlines. (We will explore this topic in the final chapter.) Taking such a Quantum Leap often calls for spinning-off the venture into a new business or brand. So how can you produce pioneering ideas within the parameters?

'Radically improve the Four Ps in the total Service Package,' is the advice given by Barrie Hopson and Mike Scally, authors of *12 Steps To Success Through Service*. Their concept is covered in my earlier books, so here is just a brief introduction to the Four Ps.

- The **Product**: This is the basic product or service you offer customers.
- The **People Skills**: These are the people skills that you employ when carrying out your work.

- The **Procedures**: This means organising your procedures to put the customer first, rather than last, such as making it easy for them to do business with you.
- The **Packaging**: This is the way you present your product or service to the customer. Hopson and Scally suggest concrete ways you can improve each part of the Service Package.

Imagination is crucial. Bearing this in mind, how do you personally develop fresh ideas? Do you visualise pictures; study positive models; follow a certain mental process; brainstorm possibilities; dialogue with friends; play music; go for a walk, read books or whatever? Try tackling the exercise called *My Creative Breakthroughs*. Describe a time when you took an imaginative leap; what you did right then; and how to apply similar methods when exercising your brain. Creativity will help to make full use of your talents, which leads to the final step taken by people who continually deliver brilliance.

The Service Package

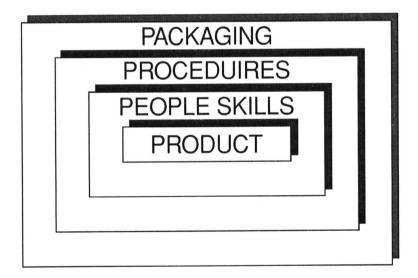

PACKAGING
PROCEDUIRES
PEOPLE SKILLS
PRODUCT

CLASS: You can add that touch of class

Great chefs, singers and footballers all add that extra touch of class. They present a meal beautifully; sing a memorable encore; or score with an acrobatic overhead kick. On a scale 0-10, rate yourself on having the ability to add this special quality in your chosen field.

Nelson Mandela demonstrated this gift when departing from a famous hotel in London. His plane for Johannesburg left early from Heathrow, which meant a 6am departure from the hotel. Walking across the reception area, he noticed a row of employees waiting to see if they could help. Breaking away from his entourage, Mandela walked towards the waiting line. He shook hands with each person, thanking them for looking after him during his stay. Only after completing his goodbyes did he climb into the waiting limousine and embark on his journey. Nelson Mandela showed a touch of class.

How can you continue to perform superb work? Try tackling the second part of the exercise called *Becoming A Class Act*. Describe the specific steps you can take to improve in the areas of Character, Competence, Consistency, Creativity and Class. Soon it will be time to roll up your sleeves and sweat. Before then, however, let's explore how you can get encouragement when following your vocation.

137

CONTINUITY AND CREATIVITY

Class Acts get the right balance between Continuity and Creativity. They make sure that: (a) They keep the right things; (b) They develop or change the right things. This exercise invites you to focus on these issues in your work place.

CONTINUITY
The areas of my work where it is important for me to provide continuity are:

- _____
- _____
- _____
- _____

CREATIVITY
The areas of my work where I can be creative are:

- _____
- _____
- _____
- _____

MY CREATIVE BREAKTHROUGHS

A time when I made a creative breakthrough was:

● when _____

The things I did to create the breakthrough were:

● _____

● _____

● _____

The principles I believe I may follow for making creative breakthroughs are:

1. to _____

2. to _____

3. to _____

The steps I can take to follow these principles in the future are:

1. to _____

2. to _____

3. to _____

BECOMING A CLASS ACT (2)

Try tackling this exercise that invites you to focus on how you can improve your performance in your chosen field.

CHARACTER
How I can continue to develop the right attitude and character needed to succeed in my chosen field

● I can _____

● I can _____

● I can _____

COMPETENCE
How I can continue to develop the right skills and competence required to succeed in my chosen field

● I can _____

● I can _____

● I can _____

CONSISTENCY
How I can continue to develop the consistency required
to succeed in my chosen field

- I can _____

- I can _____

- I can _____

CREATIVITY
How I can continue to develop and apply the creativity
required to succeed in my chosen field

- I can _____

- I can _____

- I can _____

CLASS
How I can continue to add that extra 'touch of class'
required to succeed in my chosen field

- I can _____

- I can _____

- I can _____

Support

'Sticking with the mountaineering analogy, my boss and I agreed that I should climb Everest,' reported one person. 'But the practical help was not forthcoming. Scaling Ben Nevis would have been a more realistic target. Then I would not have frozen on the glacier.'

Sounds familiar? Two things are worth remembering. First, be sure to get the support contract agreed up-front. Second, be clear on the support you can and can't expect from an employer. People often say things like: 'I would like recognition from the company.' Sad to say, in most businesses, any praise you get will be a bonus. Bosses seldom walk the floor dispensing positive strokes. Some do, but they are the exception. You will probably have to supply your own encouragement to fuel the journey. Here are some suggestions.

You can get the agreed support

Dave, the football manager, discovered that his new club delivered on their promises. Soccer clubs rise or fall depending on the quality of certain key relationships; one of them being between the Chairman and manager. The Chairman rang him everyday to see what practical help could be provided. Dave recruited his backroom team from other clubs, which involved paying hefty compensation, and was given large funds for new players. Sounds ideal? Yes; but Dave then recognised it was up to him to deliver the goods. How can you get the agreed support to do your job, be it financial, practical or emotional?

Start the ball rolling by proactively keeping your key sponsor informed. This is much more effective than haranguing, complaining or confronting. Take the initiative by giving regular up-to-date progress reports. Providing you produce early successes, and show the overall state of play, they are more likely to say: 'That sounds good. Is there any help you want?' Give them 'certainty' and avoid nasty surprises. Sometimes it is easy to neglect this skill of managing upwards.

'I nearly got the sack during my probation period with a new company,' reported Kevin, a sale person. 'My style is to be the Lone

Ranger. Back in my previous company, I spent weeks on the road visiting customers, reporting to Head Office every three months. In my new company, the unspoken rule was that I must keep my managers informed. I nearly blew it, because my mistaken approach was: 'I will produce my first big sale like a rabbit out of the hat.''

'The turnaround came just in time. Somebody advised me to imagine that I was a freelancer on a three-month rolling contract. If my next order depended on the key internal managers signing off the cheque, would I behave differently? My reply: 'Of course. I would get even more sales and also keep the decision-makers informed on a daily basis.' The penny dropped. Within two weeks of adopting this approach, I was offered a permanent position.'

Be proactive and positive. You are more likely to get the agreed practical support by sharing your successes, and the challenges ahead, rather than by complaining. Needless to say, do not become a victim or a suffering martyr. If the funding, staff recruitment or autonomy is not forthcoming, then consider your position. But make sure you have an alternative. This will add strength to your stance.

You can get support from other people

Spend time with Encouragers, rather than with Stoppers. Great workers tend to be self-starters who love their vocation. At the same time, however, they surround themselves with people who are stimulating. Try tackling the exercise called *My Self-Confidence Pot*, which was devised by Virginia Satir, a great family therapist. Start by drawing an imaginary pot (see illustration.) Then go through the following steps.

Step 1: Looking at the pot, draw a line that corresponds with how high you feel your self-confidence is today. If you have high confidence, draw it high up the pot. If your confidence is low, draw the line at a lower point in the pot. Now let's consider why it may be at this level.

Step 2: Write the names of the 'Pot Fillers.' These are the people in your life who put encouragement and energy into your pot. Similarly, you might do things yourself to put such ingredients into your pot. If you get masses of support, then 'your cup will run over', and you will pass-on encouragement to other people. But there may be complications, which brings us to the next part of the exercise.

Step 3: Write the names of the 'Pot Drillers.' For example, Discouragers and Energy Drainers. The more significant they are in your life, the nearer they will be to the base. Similarly, you may do things to drill holes in your own pot. For example, one athlete had a painful script, continually criticising himself with negative self-talk after competitions. While self-development is crucial, he devoted 90% of his energy to focusing on his failures. One other point – some people may be both Pot Fillers and Pot Drillers. For example, they may have a 'Pleasing-Hurting' pattern. Sometimes they are positive then, without warning, they lash out. Clarify the specific things they do to support or stop you.

How to use this information? Holes in the bottom of the pot mean you will struggle to maintain the same level of confidence. Encouragement might flow in the top, but it will drain away, sapping your energy. So what are the solutions? The Basic Rules are simple.

MY SELF-CONFIDENCE POT

How high is your self-confidence? Looking at the imaginary pot, draw a line that corresponds with how high your self-confidence is today. For example, if you have high confidence, draw it high up the pot. If your confidence is low, then draw it at an appropriate level. Then write the names of the Pot Fillers, the Pot Drillers and those who do both.

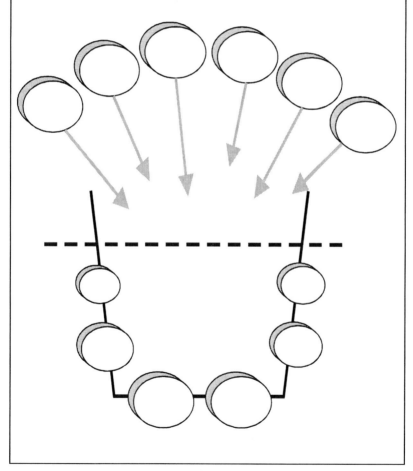

POT FILLERS

The people who put encouragement and energy into my pot are:

- _____
- _____
- _____

- _____
- _____
- _____

The things I do to put encouragement and energy into my pot are:

- _____
- _____
- _____

- _____
- _____
- _____

POT DRILLERS

The people who discourage me or take energy away are:

- _____
- _____
- _____

- _____
- _____
- _____

The things I do to discourage myself or take energy away are:

- _____
- _____
- _____

- _____
- _____
- _____

MY ACTION PLAN

The specific things I can do to put encouragement and energy into my pot are:

- to _____
- to _____
- to _____

The specific things I can do to fill the holes in my pot are:

- to _____
- to _____
- to _____

Rule 1 – Spend more time with people who give you energy.

Energy is Life: so do the things that give you energy. Start by getting close to your Encouragers. If possible, only work with colleagues you find stimulating. Many people often find that, as they get older, they spend more time with personal and professional soul mates. Prevention is better than cure, so how to increase your zest for life? Devote time to the experiences you find invigorating, such as listening to music, skiing, sailing, visiting the theatre or whatever. Pursuing these activities will put more energy into your pot.

Rule 2 – Spend less time – or no time – with people who drain energy.

Radical changes are difficult to make overnight but, unless the holes are filled, encouragement will simply flow out of the bottom. So how to deal with Stoppers? You can do two things.

● Stop seeing people who drain energy. Not always possible straight away, but it may be feasible in the long term. Why take this drastic step? Spending time with somebody who abuses you, for instance, is rewarding their behaviour. The answer is to physically move away; otherwise you become a victim. But what if you want to maintain some aspects of a relationship with people who give double-messages?

● Start making clear contracts with the people who both encourage and stop you. (a) Reward the positive. Give clear messages about the specific things you do like them doing. Explain how you would like to build on these parts of the relationship. (b) Give positive alternatives to the negative. Explain that: 'In the future, is it possible for you to ....' or 'I would prefer it if you ...' Present suggestions, rather than label them as 'bad'. Don't expect people to respond immediately; everybody needs time to lick their wounds. Don't argue or fall into the blame game. What if the person refuses to respond? Then make the decision whether to stay or leave.

Finally – when in doubt, ask yourself: 'Is this activity giving me energy?' If not, switch to spending time with the people, and on the activities, that provide stimulation. Positive energy is the source of life, which leads to the next step.

You can support yourself

Start by playing to your strengths. 'Now I do what I do best,' said Helen, an Account Director. 'One year ago, I re-crafted my career to make full use of my talents. My best work is done by acting as a 'confidante' to customers, who are decision makers in leading-edge companies. Looking at the challenges they face, we explore possible solutions. Frequently they want customised solutions that fit their needs, rather than commodity packages. Sometimes, I provide products from my own company; sometimes, I recommend other solutions. My role is to maintain the relationship and help them succeed. Paradoxically, my sales have increased.'

Spend time with customers and colleagues who you find stimulating. Helen enjoyed working with Directors who were quick, bright and demanding. 'Middle managers drive me crazy,' she said. 'They often have an investment in making the world complicated and never making a decision. Give me somebody who can sign a cheque, rather than schedule another meeting.' She likes working alongside colleagues who share similar values, people whom, in her words, 'Get it'. Do you work best with certain kinds of customers and colleagues? If so, what are their characteristics? How can you devote more time to being with such people?

Spend time in your sanctuaries. Everybody needs a place where they can relax, re-centre and refocus. Where do you feel at peace? Where do you go to make sense of the world? Try tackling the exercise called *My Sanctuaries*. Perhaps you have a favourite place in your garden; like to walk in the woods; or visit particular soul mates. Spending time in sanctuaries offers the chance to rise above daily tasks and see things in perspective. You can then make good quality decisions about shaping your future.

Spend time employing a creative outlet. World events can be depressing and put poison into your system. Bearing in mind the 'Input-Output' model, what goes in must come out. So it is helpful to translate any negative energy you experience into something positive. Try tackling the exercise called *My Creative Outlet.* You may choose to express your feelings through painting, writing, gardening, designing, playing music or whatever. Getting the right balance between 'input' and 'output' increases the chances of enjoying a healthy life.

Support gives fuel for the journey. Now it is time to move onto the final stage. Let's explore how to fulfil your vocation and perform valuable work.

MY SANCTUARIES

My sanctuaries are:

- _____

- _____

- _____

The benefit of spending time in these sanctuaries is:

- _____

- _____

- _____

My plans for making full use of these sanctuaries are:

- _____

- _____

- _____

MY CREATIVE OUTLETS

My creative outlets are:

- _____
- _____
- _____

The benefits of employing these creative outlets are:

- _____
- _____
- _____

My plans for making more creative use of these outlets are:

- _____
- _____
- _____

STEP THREE
VALUABLE WORK

Fulfilling Your Vocation

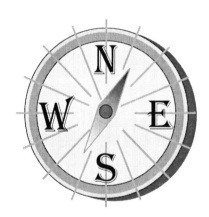

THE
MAGIC
OF
WORK

*How you can balance your
Soul Work and Salary Work*

Introduction

'When you have completed 80% of the job, there is only 80% left,' is a good guideline. Time to work hard, which is the enjoyable part. Certainly I have found this to be true when writing books. While wanting to 'ship the product', I almost prefer the daily ritual of putting together each page. People are sometimes classified as *architects*, who design the house; *builders*, who erect the house; or *craftsmen*, who engrave each brick. Sometimes we play all three roles, especially when following our calling. Sometimes this is possible to achieve alone. Other times we need colleagues who add their complementary talents to help us succeed.

Finishing is a skill we learn early in life. As a child, you may have loved inventing games, painting pictures, writing stories, building engines or whatever. The theory is simple: 'Flow, Focus, Finish,' and, as a by-product, 'Find Fulfilment.' Sounds straightforward, but the terrain can be complicated. How to learn from your past experiences? Try the exercise called *My Finishing Skills*. Looking back over the years, describe something you have completed in your personal or professional life. It can be tangible, such as completing a book, or something such as moving on from a relationship. What did you do right on that occasion? Describe how you can apply these skills to your latest adventure.

'Enjoy the journey as much as reaching the goal,' is the maxim. How to put this advice into practice? How to focus on your picture of perfection? How to remain calm during a crisis? The following pages go through the stages of *Sweat, Solutions, Sharing Knowledge* and *Success*. Let's explore these steps towards doing valuable work.

MY FINISHING SKILLS

(a) Describe a time when you have finished something successfully. This can be in your personal or professional life. It could have been something tangible, such as completing a book or a project, or perhaps something such as moving on from a relationship.

● When I _____

(b) Describe what you did right to complete it successfully

● I _____

● I _____

● I _____

● I _____

● I _____

(c) How can you follow these principles again in the future? If you wish, focus on a particular challenge. Describe the specific steps you can take to finish it successfully

● _____

● _____

● _____

Sweat

When do you sweat? Not just physically, but creatively? Satisfying sweat comes from thriving in your element and striving to achieve a meaningful goal. Feeling shattered at night, you enjoy an exhilarating tiredness. Disillusionment comes from performing work that is alien to your values. Try tackling the exercise called *Satisfying Sweat*. 'I love exploring the frontiers of science,' explained one researcher. 'Hours can go by without me noticing the clock. I am swept away by the joy of gathering information and discovering new patterns. Living on this cliff-edge becomes a positive addiction. Sometimes it is hard to go home at night to a more mundane life.' Work can be a real soul mate, so how can you fulfil your labour of love?

You can keep following the right way

'Keep doing the right things in the right way every day to get the right results,' is the mantra. Peak performers develop a rhythm and repeat good habits. Staying in shape is more effective than falling into bad habits and having to 'fight the flab.' Regaining momentum can be difficult, especially if your hard work fails to produce instant results.

'My diary is empty at the moment,' reported John, a consultant who telephoned me one February. 'While I understand the theory of winning business through networking, it is taking ages for people to get back into the swing after Christmas. Any suggestions?'

John's business had been booming during the previous autumn. Feeling secure, he took a long skiing vacation from mid November to early December. The knock-on effect was losing touch with clients for over two months. Now it was a hard slog to revive his network. Looking back, John acknowledged he should have delayed his vacation until everybody took holidays. Now he must knuckle down and contact people.

Frustrated that he was failing to see instant results, John even considered taking a steady job in corporate life. One month devoted to nurturing the seeds in his network, however, saw the first glimmers of 'spring flowers'. John's diary began to fill up with new workshops.

Try tackling the exercise called *The Right Way*. Start by focusing on your picture of perfection. Then describe how you can do the right things in the right way every day to get these results. Sticking to these daily disciplines provides the greatest chance of achieving success. Disappointments will surface along the way, however, which calls for demonstrating resilience. Let's explore how to overcome unexpected problems.

You can manage setbacks

How do you bounce back from shocks? A customer cancels the contract, leaving a hole in your income; the publisher returns your book, wishing you luck in the future; your key sponsor departs the company, leaving your project hanging by a thread. *The Survivor Personality* by Al Siebert and *Adversity Quotient @ Work* by Paul Gordon Stoltz are two fine books that provide maps for overcoming traumas. Try tackling the exercise called *Managing Setbacks*, which explores your way of recovering. Some people become frenzied, like the golfer who hacks away in the rough, searching for the magic shot to restore his fortunes. The alternative is to follow proven steps for surviving difficulties.

You can work through the reactive change curve

Sweat of a different kind is called for when tackling unexpected suffering. When such events occur, we often travel through the classic *Reactive Change Curve* (see illustration). Here are some of the stages we may experience on the road to recovery.

SATISFYING SWEAT

The times when I experience satisfying sweat are:

- When I am _____

- When I am _____

- When I am _____

The specific things I am doing right then are:

- _____

- _____

- _____

The steps I can take to do more of these things are:

- _____

- _____

- _____

THE RIGHT WAY

THE RIGHT RESULTS
The results I am aiming to achieve are:

- to _____
- to _____
- to _____

THE RIGHT THINGS
The right things I can do each day are:

- to _____
- to _____
- to _____

THE RIGHT WAY
The right way I can do these things is:

- to _____
- to _____
- to _____

MANAGING SETBACKS

(1)   Describe a setback you have experienced in your life that you managed successfully.

When I _____

_____

(2)   Describe what you did right to overcome the setback.

- I _____

- I _____

- I _____

- I _____

- I _____

How can you use what you learned? Describe three concrete things you can do to manage setbacks in the future.

- I can _____

- I can _____

- I can _____

The Reactive Change Curve

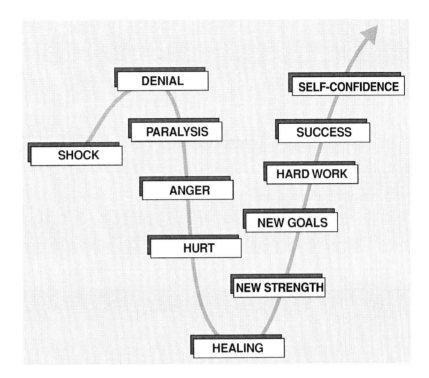

Shock

People experience a crisis. They lose their job, suffer an accident or witness a disaster. Shock is the first reaction to trauma, whether somebody has got the sack, been involved in a car accident, lost a loved one or got caught in a disaster, such as being crushed at the Hillsborough football ground. Shock gives way to the next stage.

Denial

A feeling of unreality follows: 'It's not true. It can't be happening. I can't believe it'. Authorities at Hillsborough denied there was a crowd problem – they wanted to get on with the semi-final. A driver climbs out of a smashed car, insists he feels all right and wants to continue his journey. A patient hears she has an incurable disease, but insists the hospital has mixed-up the x-rays. Political leaders insist: 'Everything is fine,' when confronted by a crisis, such as BSE or Chernobyl.

Paralysis

The police froze at Hillsborough. Constables reported that they had been ordered to stop spectators getting onto the pitch whatever the circumstances. Distressed fans were therefore herded back into pens that had become death traps. Crucial minutes were lost before they evacuated spectators trapped behind the terrace barriers. Paralysis is common in many stress situations. Bureaucrats in threatened organisations continue to follow old procedures, hoping the dangers will disappear. Passengers relax on planes that have crash-landed successfully, thinking their ordeal is over, only to be overcome by toxic fumes.

Anger

'Let's find somebody to blame,' is the cry, as people search for scapegoats. Victims pin blame on, for example, the police, the football authorities, political parties, the other car driver, the airline pilot or God. Some blame Life that has treated them cruelly. People often need to vent their feelings and experience a catharsis before entering the next stage.

Hurt

Pain seeps through the body, the organisation or the nation. Tears are shed; nightmares are re-lived. Individuals react differently: some talk; some sleep; some drink; some retreat into silence; some relapse into depression. Many people feel they are sinking downwards and fear they won't pull-out of the dive. They come to terms with the pain, however, and enter the next stage.

Healing

The optimistic scenario: the body recovers, the mind begins to understand. Full acceptance takes longer, but it is time to start on the road to recovery. The pessimistic scenario is that people sink deeper and experience a breakdown. Some stay at this level all their lives. While it is vital to encourage people, they must also take responsibility for their own future. Most people pull the pieces together and decide that life must go on, which takes us to the next step.

New Strength

People emerge from mourning as the mind searches for deeper meaning. The 45 year-old who has experienced a heart attack, for example, considers giving up a stressful job and developing a healthier life-style. The physical and psychological strength needed to tackle future challenges are mobilised. The body feels stronger, the mind more determined: it is time to get out of bed and translate the feelings into actions.

New Goals

After a painful divorce, a person aims to start a new relationship. After surviving an air accident, a traveller plans a new air trip. After the Hillsborough disaster, some football clubs removed the fencing while others procrastinated; eventually they were all forced to revamp their stadiums. After a crippling earthquake, a shattered population vow to re-build their homes. People need a long-term vision, but must also set short-term realistic goals that will produce visible successes.

Hard Work

People start fresh relationships, find new jobs, re-build a city or re-construct a nation after a disaster. Nothing can replace the hard work required. Sweat has a cleansing effect: people feel they are doing something and begin to see results. (Some may relapse at this point, returning to Anger and Hurt.) The next step is to translate the action into some early wins.

Success

Some Liverpool fans felt better after attending their first post-Hillsborough match, others still felt troubled. A sacked worker feels better after completing her first week in a new job. A divorced person feels better after developing a more enriching relationship. Earthquake victims feel better after clearing the ruins and erecting the first houses: they feel even more determined to re-build their city. People cannot be given success; they have to earn it. They can be offered the right encouragement and tools to do the job, but they must get out of the chair and do the work.

Self-Confidence

People put the bad experience into perspective. Some may be bitter, others have different reactions, such as: 'It was the best thing that ever happened to me. It taught me that I could survive anything. It made me appreciate life and concentrate on my priorities.' They feel older, wiser and stronger.

How do you behave after a setback? As we mentioned earlier, one of the keys is to develop the daily rhythm of doing the right things in the right way. Results do not necessarily appear overnight. Providing you do what you know works, the fruits of your labours will blossom in the future.

You can just do it

'Actors act, painters paint, writers write, inventors invent and musicians make music,' said one of my teachers. ''Shapers' do what they want to do to shape the world. 'Sleepers' wait until the world has changed to give them the chance to follow their dream. What type are you?' Try tackling the exercise called *Just Do It*, which invites you to implement your action plans. Then follow the daily disciplines required to deliver. Pursuing your adventure will bring both pleasure and problems. As we have seen in this section, sometimes you may need to simply work your way through crises. Good navigators often anticipate such challenges, however, which leads us to the next step.

JUST DO IT!

My first goal is:

● _____

My action plan is:

● to _____ ☐

● to _____ ☐

● to _____ ☐

My second goal is:

● _____

My action plan is:

● to _____ ☐

● to _____ ☐

● to _____ ☐

My third goal is:

● _____

My action plan is:

● to _____ ☐

● to _____ ☐

● to _____ ☐

Solutions

'Entrepreneurs are big risk-takers. Right?' Not the successful ones, says Peter Drucker, the management guru. Such pioneers do not fit the stereotype of their being gamblers. Possessing strong control needs, they are like mountain climbers. They follow a dream, but have a contingency plan for every foreseeable eventuality. Isn't it still a risk to climb the mountain? Yes – but refusing the call would be a greater existential risk. They could not live with themselves if they failed to strive for the summit. Before setting out, however, they create back-up plans for managing possible difficulties. Let's explore how you can adopt this approach in your work.

You can anticipate potential sticky moments

Imagine you have been invited to set-up an On-Line Banking Service for a traditional High Street Bank. Specific goals have been agreed with your sponsor, who is a go-ahead type in a stuffy establishment. The Bank's customer service policies still leave much to be desired, but it has reluctantly decided to enter the 21st Century. The Senior Team headhunted an outside candidate to implement the new approach. After trawling through dynamic financial service companies, your sponsor was captured. Having collaborated with you before on a similar assignment, he invited you to lead the team that would introduce On-Line banking. You recognise the danger signals, but still decide to accept the project.

Good navigators chart the route to success, but also anticipate possible problems. How to apply this approach when implementing the On-Line service? Gather your team together and tackle the exercise called *Managing Sticky Moments*. Ask them: 'Looking ahead at what we must achieve, what may be the potentially difficult situations?'

Brainstorm the scenarios, for example: 'The Bank may pull the plug on the project. The key sponsor may leave or be fired. The key stakeholders may try to sabotage the project. The budget may get slashed. The members in our team may not gel. The system may crash on the first day. The security screen may be breached.'

Time to move onto solutions. Get the team members to break into groups, each tackling one of the issues. Ask them to return in an hour and make a presentation on:

(a) THE POTENTIAL DIFFICULTY. The potentially difficult situation is …

(b) PREVENTION. The specific things we can do to prevent the situation happening are …

c) MANAGEMENT. The specific things we can do to manage the situation if it does happen are …

d) POSITIVE POSSIBILITIES. The positive possibilities that might emerge if the situation does happen are …

Why invite people to consider such problems? The obvious reason is to find solutions, but it is also important to build the team's 'Collective Radar'. Educating people to mentally rehearse managing difficulties increases their ability to make decisions without relying on your guidance. You will also find some surprising positive possibilities emerge. (Four years ago I met a high tech team in the City. They lived with the ever-present danger of their employer closing their project, but reframed it as being paid to pilot the know-how. If the company called it a day, they would then launch the product themselves. Six months later this actually happened. After negotiating a deal with the previous employer, they built a thriving business.) Anticipating problems is one side of the coin, but the flip side is also worth considering.

You can anticipate potential successes

'Rehearsing how to build on success is as vital as coping with setbacks,' explained Dave, the football manager, who took a strong interest in sports psychology. 'Leading 2-0 early in a match brings is own problems. Players can start to 'showboat', refusing to ram home their advantage. Declaring victory too early, they get hit by the sucker punch. Suddenly the opposition gains momentum and you lose control of the game.'

How to capitalise on your wins? This is a tantalising quandary, especially if you run a one-person firm. Customers will often be buying your knowledge. Countless individual suppliers have tried to increase profits by hiring employees, only to discover the new people do not share the same high standards. Try tackling the exercise called *Managing Potential Successes.* Describe how to build on your achievements. 'Just put up your prices,' argue some advisers. Yes, this is one possibility. Another is to devote more attention to stimulating customers, while spending less time with those who drain energy. Let's move onto another serious challenge that demands creative solutions.

You can recognise and beat the 'double bind'

Have you ever been in a double bind? These are situations where, no matter what you do, you are bound to lose. A child used as a pawn between rowing parents, for example, will feel they cannot win. In the worst scenario, the mother says: 'If you love me more than your father, come to me.' Father says: 'If you love me more than your mother, come to me.' The child has an impossible choice. Showing favour to one parent will incur the wrath of the other. Both options are painful. Retreating into the child's own world is often the only salvation.

Double binds also occur in our relationships at work. A strong signal that you are entering such territory is when you feel a knot in your stomach. Something happened – either between you and a manager, in a meeting, or elsewhere – which makes you feel uneasy. Examining the situation in more detail, you find that you have been placed in a position where, whatever you do, you are bound to lose. (Some people even put themselves in double binds. For example, they use 50% of their energy thinking of a positive way forward in their lives; then employ the other 50% knocking it down by worrying about what can go wrong. Confusing? Yes, but some people experience this inner dialogue.)

Clear contracting is the best way to untangle the double bind. Start by contracting within yourself: clarify what you do and don't want to do in the situation. Then make clear contracts with other people. For example, imagine you normally spend Christmas holidays with your parents. Looking back on previous festive visits, they normally start well, then lapse into boredom. September arrives and they will phone any day, inviting you for two weeks. Prepare your reply: 'I am happy to come for two days. Then my partner and I are going to take a break overseas in the sunshine.' 'But I have already ordered the turkey,' may be the response. Stand firm. Tough perhaps, but it is one way to move forward in the relationship.

How to manage such conflicts? Try tackling the exercise called *Beating The Double Bind*. First, describe where you may experience a 'No Win' situation. Second, describe the factors that mean that, whatever you do, you are likely to lose. Third, describe steps you can take to beat the double bind. Prevention is normally better than cure, so try to make clear contracts before going into difficult situations. What if this is not possible? Choose the route forward that will, in the long term, cause the least pain. Survivors often develop the 'Radar' to spot double binds when these appear on the horizon. They recognise that avoiding such pain can save lots of energy.

MANAGING POTENTIAL STICKY MOMENTS

THE POTENTIAL DIFFICULTY IS:

- _____

PREVENTION - The specific things I can do to prevent the difficulty happening are:

- _____

- _____

- _____

MANAGEMENT - The specific things I can do to manage the difficulty if it happens are:

- _____

- _____

- _____

POSITIVE POSSIBILITIES - The positive possibilities that may emerge from the difficulty are:

- _____

- _____

- _____

MANAGING POTENTIAL SUCCESSES

THE POTENTIAL SUCCESSES ARE:

(a) _____

(b) _____

(c) _____

BUILDING ON SUCCESS

The specific ways I can build on each of these successes are:

(a) to _____

(b) to _____

(c) to _____

BEATING THE DOUBLE BIND

(1) Describe a present or future situation where you believe you may experience a double bind.

● _____

_____

(2) Describe the factors that mean that, whatever you do, you are likely to lose. For example, if you do A, the outcome will be _____; if you do B, the outcome will be _____.

● _____

_____

● _____

_____

(3) Describe the specific things you can do to make sure you beat the double bind.

● I can _____

● I can _____

● I can _____

You can manage crises successfully

How will you react to crises that throw you off-course? Looking back at the *Reactive Change Curve*, there are various emotional stages people must go through to overcome traumas. But what can you do on a practical level? Let's explore one model for managing personal or professional crises (see illustration).

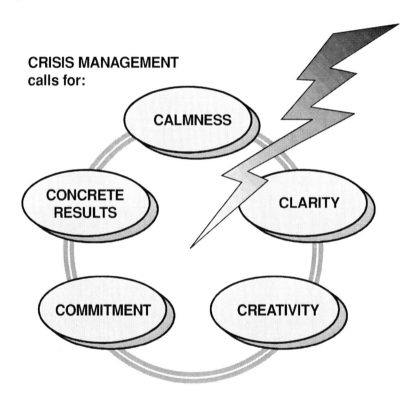

CRISIS MANAGEMENT calls for:

CALMNESS

CONCRETE RESULTS

CLARITY

COMMITMENT

CREATIVITY

Step 1: CALMNESS

Stay calm. Get an overview and see things in perspective. Things may not be as bad as they seem. On the other hand, they may be much worse! Whether you are arriving at an accident scene, counselling a troubled person or recovering from a mistake, quickly grasp the big picture. Start by identifying the key challenges to tackle. Bear one thing in mind – while immediate actions may need to be taken, these must also fit with the long-term goal. For example, moving an injured person can cause internal damage. Similarly, governmental knee-jerk 'solutions' to traffic problems can store-up difficulties for later years. Get all the information, then move onto the next step.

Step 2: CLARITY

Clarify the 'Real Results' to achieve. Arriving at an accident scene, the immediate priority may be to ease the victim's pain. Longer term, the goal is to enable them to make a full recovery. Counselling a recently laid-off employee may carry them through the short-term trauma. If the person has a pattern of getting fired, however, you will need to establish whether they want to keep drifting or shape their future destiny? Clarity about the long-term goal is crucial; you can then move onto the next stage.

Step 3: CREATIVITY

'Necessity is the mother of invention,' we are told. Crises can give birth to imaginative solutions. Looking at the real results to achieve, what are all the possible things you can do to reach these goals? First, consider all the 'conventional' ways. Tried and trusted methods may already exist for tackling this problem. Second, consider all the 'creative' ways. For example, 'Child Line' was invented to enable young abuse victims to ring for help. Call Centres were established on different continents to provide round the clock customer service. Whatever crisis you face, there are both conventional and creative means to reach the goal. Clarify the pluses and minuses of pursuing each route; then make your choice. (You may adopt parallel strategies. Some tackle the short-term issues, while others address the longer-term goals.) This leads to the next step.

Step 4: COMMITMENT

Once you have made your choice, go for it 100%. Commitment is a relatively straightforward process for individuals who, for example, decide to repay debts, stay sober or regain their health. They must then work at it every day. Super Teams also fully commit themselves to achieving the shared goals. Complications can arise in teams, however, because some people may prefer other options or have other agendas. Sometimes it is still possible to get win-wins. One solution is to form smaller teams, each pursuing their own methods, providing they work in a complementary fashion towards the shared goals. (Sounds difficult, but scientific research for medical cures often follows this model.) Sweat is then required to reach the picture of perfection.

Step 5: CONCRETE RESULTS

Success is achieved. The road crash victim recovers; the discarded employee finds a new job; the railway company fulfils its revamped timetable. Good crisis management calls for going further, however, and applying the key learning points. Farming catastrophes, such as BSE and Foot & Mouth Disease, contain lessons that can be used to establish healthier food practice. Disasters can be caused by an 'Act of God', but they also provide pointers towards building a better future. Try tackling the exercise called *Crisis Management*. Doing valuable work unearths new solutions to problems, which bring knowledge. Time to pass on your wisdom.

CRISIS MANAGEMENT

CALMNESS - the steps I can take to stay calm in a crisis are:

- to _____

- to _____

CLARITY - the steps I can take to be clear on the results I want to achieve are:

- to _____

- to _____

CREATIVITY - the steps I can take to explore both the creative and conventional routes are:

- to _____

- to _____

COMMITMENT - the steps I can take to fully commit myself to the course of action are:

- to _____

- to _____

CONCRETE RESULTS - the steps I can take to get concrete results are:

- to _____

- to _____

Sharing knowledge

'My 50th birthday lit the fuse,' explained Birgitta, a dentist who practices in Berlin. 'Maybe I became aware of mortality, but suddenly I felt the desire to pass on my philosophy about Odontology. State funding for dentists is geared to fixing problems, but many in our profession prefer to work on prevention. So I decided to share this approach with younger dentists.

'The local university hires me to address dental students once a month as a visiting lecturer. Talking to big groups is not satisfying, so I invite six students to eat dinner afterwards at an Italian restaurant. The students submit questions beforehand and, between pasta courses, I try to answer them. Queries range from technical matters concerning Odontology to practical issues involved in running a surgery. The students tell me about their lives and sometimes it seems like I am the one who is learning.'

Age provides many lessons. What knowledge can you convey to other people? How can you communicate these messages? Do you feel comfortable writing, teaching, coaching or employing some other vehicle? With whom can you share your ideas – everybody or a specific target group? What will be the benefits? Let's consider different methods of transmitting your know-how.

You can clarify 'what' you want to pass on to people

Imagine you have been invited to address a group of 18 year-olds. You have five minutes to share your wisdom. What three key messages would you give the young people? Perhaps you would prefer to address aspiring professionals in your own field. What expertise would you like to impart? Everybody has learned lessons in their lives, even if it has been the art of survival. Try tackling the exercise called *Passing On Knowledge*. Bearing in mind your strengths, start by identifying the tools in your kit bag. For example, you may be able to help people to learn:

- how to survive school
- how to develop their natural gifts – for example, the ability to draw, paint, sculpt, play sports, write software or whatever
- how to master a particular skill – for example, the ability to start a business, make presentations, manage people, build great teams or whatever
- how to succeed by going around the system
- how to cope with adversity
- how to enjoy getting older.

Clarify your offering by completing the following. 'The knowledge I can pass on to people is:

- how to _____

- how to _____

- how to _____

You can clarify 'how' you want to pass on your knowledge to people

What is the best vehicle for sharing your wisdom? You may be in your element as a keynote speaker, writer, leader, coach, professional specialist or whatever. You may prefer to work with individuals, small groups or large audiences. Looking back on your life, tackle the exercise called *My Positive Teacher*. How did this person transmit know-how? Great educators often follow the Three Is: Inspiration, Implementation and Integration. They create an inspiring environment where motivated people can learn; provide implementation tools that work; and help people to integrate the learning into their personal or professional lives. How can you be a good teacher, mentor or coach?

MY POSITIVE TEACHER

(1) Looking back on your life, write the name of somebody who, for you, has been a positive teacher. He or she might have been a teacher in school. On the other hand, it could have been a leader, manager, sports coach or whatever. Write the person's name.

● _____

(2) What did he or she do right to be a good teacher? Describe the specific things done to help you learn

● He/she _____

● He/she _____

● He/she _____

● He/she _____

● He/she _____

(3) How can you follow these principles your own way? Describe three things you can do to pass on knowledge and help others to learn.

● I can _____

● I can _____

● I can _____

Dave, the soccer manager, has chosen to help hungry athletes to make full use of their gifts. One of the 'new breed' of managers who are making their mark in the game, he is far removed from the old-style boss who everybody called 'Gaffer'. Football managers are often seen as falling into one of three categories.

Enthusiasts: They are energetic cheerleaders who try to gee-up players with 'Gung-ho' speeches before the kick-off and at half-time.

Enforcers: They demand that players fit into their preferred system. While discipline is necessary, such managers sometimes come across as having the 'factory boss' mentality.

Educators: They see the game through the eyes of an educator. When watching the match unfold, they ask themselves: 'How can this player, or the team, improve by: a) Building on their strengths? b) Tackling other areas for development?' They then ask themselves: 'How can I put this message in a way the players can receive?'

Dave is a mixture of all three. His ratings would be: Enthusiast 9/10; Enforcer 7/10; Educator 9/10. He realises that, in the past, some players saw him as 'soft touch'. During the past two years, however, he has set clear guidelines on behaviour and acted accordingly if these were broken. The activity he loves most is helping players to develop, both on and off the training ground. During his early 20s, Dave recognised his ability was limited, so he began studying for coaching badges. Managing a football club is, for him, the best job in the world. What is your preferred vehicle for sharing know-how?

You can clarify 'why' you want to pass on knowledge

Artists try to cheat death by creating something that can live for eternity. Not everybody can produce a painting, book or symphony, but everybody has know-how that can benefit future generations. Certainly we stand on the shoulders of those who have gone before us. The stages of life involve: 'Living, Learning, Loving, Labouring and

Leaving A Legacy.' Perhaps there are deep psychological reasons 'why' we want to leave something behind, but sometimes it is simply best to look at the benefits. What will be value of passing on your wisdom? How will it help people, the business and yourself? Clarify the pluses by completing the following:

The benefits of sharing my knowledge will be:

for people

- _____
- _____

- _____
- _____

for the business

- _____
- _____

- _____
- _____

for myself

- _____
- _____

- _____
- _____

You can clarify to 'whom' you want to pass on knowledge

Joseph Campbell outlines the different approaches people use to transmit wisdom. Speaking in *Reflections On The Art Of Living*, he shows how individuals pursue their personal odyssey by 'going into the woods'. Finding the 'Grail', they long to communicate their insights. People take one of three routes on their return to the world. First, they try to share their vision, but the world does not want to know, so they retreat back to the woods, 'with a dog and a pipe.' Second, they meet resistance, become disheartened, and revert to the 'world's way'. They ask people: 'What do you want?' Putting their hard-earned learning on the back-burner, they give the world what it desires. Third, they make a living by becoming, in the broadest sense, a 'teacher'. Gaining credibility for their expertise, they pass on their message to people who are receptive. What is your model? With whom do you want to share your learning – with everybody or with a specific target group?

You can clarify 'when' you want to pass on knowledge

Generous people embrace 'Abundance Theory.' They believe that helping other people to succeed 'makes the cake bigger'. Others follow the rules of 'Scarcity Theory'. They feel the cake is small, so they must compete fiercely for their share. 'Abundance Theory sounds great, but surely you get ripped off,' is one argument. Generosity works when you give, but also concentrate on those people who give back in return: it does not mean becoming a victim. Giving also leads to growing. If you share information, then you are forced to develop fresh thinking. Jealously hanging onto old concepts clutters the space where new ideas can grow.

When can you get across your message? Writing a book, for example, will call for setting aside a block of time; while coaching can take place every day. Try tackling the exercise called *Passing On Knowledge*, which weaves together all the topics covered in this section. Sharing your knowledge is rewarding and will bear fruit, but do not neglect the main aim, which is to deliver the agreed picture of perfection. Time to refocus back on reaching your destination.

PASSING ON KNOWLEDGE

Everybody has learned lessons in their lives, even if it has just been how to survive. Bearing in mind your own strengths and skills, this exercise invites you to clarify what you can pass on to others.

WHAT - The knowledge I can pass on to people is:

- _____
- _____
- _____

HOW - The best vehicle - or vehicles - for me to use to pass on knowledge to people is:

- _____
- _____
- _____

WHY - The benefits of passing on this knowledge to people will be:

- _____

- _____

- _____

WHO - The specific people I want to pass this knowledge on to are:

- _____

- _____

- _____

WHEN - The specific steps I want to take to pass this knowledge on to people are:

- _____

- _____

- _____

Success

'Love the process as much as the prize,' is good advice regarding the art of finishing. Phil Jackson was the coach of Chicago Bulls when they dominated basketball during the 1990s. He talks about the 'short-lived nature of success.' Finishing is just another name for beginning. Winning Championships gives a short-term high, but new challenges lie around the corner, such as setting higher targets for next year. Great work often calls for loving the daily disciplines as much as lifting the Grail. So how can you be a good finisher?

Relax – be Calm, Controlled and Centred. Focus on your picture of perfection. Do the right things in the right way every day. Deliver on your promises and satisfy your sponsors. Then it is time to repeat the cycle again. Why? 'There are no safe jobs anymore, there are only projects.' Focus on the next fulfilling challenge. Keep expanding your network of potential sponsors. Look at how you can help them to succeed and agree clear contracts. Do pioneering work that is positive, professional and pacesetting. Let's explore these steps towards performing valuable work.

You can keep focusing on your picture of perfection

'Keep your eyes on the goal,' we are told. People are advised to have a vision – but what makes a vision work?

- First, it should be **Positive**. For example: 'I want to be healthy,' rather than, 'I want to stop smoking.'
- Second, it should be **Precise**. Make it extremely specific and detailed.
- Third, it should be **Possible**. As an athlete you may say, therefore, 'I want to do my personal best in the Olympic Final,' rather than, 'I will win.' Control the controllables, because you cannot control how other athletes will perform on the day.
- Fourth, it should be, in the widest sense, **Profitable**. You will be

more motivated to achieve pluses, rather than minimise minuses. Hence, it is more inspiring to focus on 'growing a business', rather than 'cutting costs.' Some pain may be acceptable, providing you know the end result will be pleasurable.

Try tackling the exercise called *The Picture Of Perfection*. Compelling visions often contain three elements that match the senses.

- **Seeing**. The vision incorporates what you will actually be seeing when you reach the destination. For instance: the results that will be delivered; how you will be behaving; etc.
- **Hearing**. The vision incorporates the actual words you will hear people saying.
- **Feeling**. The vision incorporates what you and other people will be feeling when you reach the destination. Bearing these elements in mind, describe or draw the actual things that will be happening when you have reached the Picture of Perfection.

How to measure progress? Make a map showing the milestones passed, those to be reached and the challenges to be tackled in the next weeks and months. Put the vision in a place where you can see it every day. You are then more likely to keep working towards fulfilling the picture.

THE PICTURE OF PERFECTION

Pick a date in the future. Describe or draw the actual things that will be happening when you have achieved your goals. Make sure the vision is Positive, Precise, Possible and, in the widest sense, Profitable. Also ensure it covers the senses of Seeing, Hearing and Feeling. Put this vision in a place where you can see it every day. You are then more likely to keep working towards fulfilling the picture. Here are some possible headings you might like to fill in.

SEEING - the specific results I will have delivered – and the things that will be happening – will be:

- _____

- _____

- _____

HEARING – the specific words people will be saying will be:

- _____

- _____

- _____

FEELING – the specific things I and others will be feeling will be:

- _____

- _____

- _____

You can enjoy the journey as well as reaching the goal

Great work is done with love. When tasting wholesome food, you recognise that joy is a key ingredient in the recipe. Looking at your own work, how can you enjoy the process whilst keeping your eyes on the prize? As we mentioned earlier, it is important to: 'Keep doing the right things in the right way every day.' How to translate this into practice? Much depends on whether you are working as an individual or part of a team.

Great leadership teams, for example, have people who fill the roles of Energiser, Environmentalist and Executor. Energisers provide the inspiring vision. Environmentalists provide a nurturing climate that encourages people to grow. Executors make sure the work gets done. Everybody may be a mixture of all three, but teams work best when there are clear demarcation lines. (Energisers who dip down into executing every detail can cause chaos.) Super teams ensure everybody does what they do best, which is the recipe for fine teamwork. Great individual workers tend to play all three roles simultaneously. They energise themselves by focusing on the vision; create the right environment; and enjoy executing certain daily tasks. Let's consider this final point.

Magical Performers get both the mundane and magical things right. First, they focus on the **Mundane Things**. For example, great singers practice daily to maintain their vocal range. Such tasks cannot be delegated, so they make them magical, creating rituals that bring meaning to the daily disciplines. Other mundane chores, such as arranging flights, can be assigned to other people. Second, they focus on the **Magical Things**. Revisiting their best performances, they identify what they did right and repeat these successful patterns. They also constantly explore new ideas to add to their 'repertoire'. Great singers, for example, get the right mix to create memorable performances.

How to put these principles into practice? Start by tackling the exercise called *Enjoying The Journey*. Consider all the jobs that must be completed to reach your destination. Clarify the tasks that: (a) you will enjoy doing, (b) you must do, (c) you can delegate to others. Bearing this in mind, move onto *My Daily Disciplines*. Describe what you must do each day to achieve your goal. The final exercise on this theme is *Magical Performances*. Plan how to manage the mundane and magical tasks involved in being the 'Best In Your Class.' Providing you follow good habits, the next step is likely to happen.

ENJOYING THE JOURNEY

The tasks that must be done to reach the goal are:

- _____
- _____
- _____

The tasks I will enjoy doing are:

- _____
- _____
- _____

The other tasks I must do are:

- _____
- _____
- _____

The steps I can take to enjoy doing these are:

- _____
- _____
- _____

The tasks I can delegate are:

- _____
- _____
- _____

ENJOYING THE JOURNEY - MY ACTION PLAN

The steps I can take to enjoy the journey are:

- _____
- _____
- _____

MY DAILY DISCIPLINES

The daily disciplines I must follow to reach my goal are:

- to _____

_____

- to _____

_____

- to _____

_____

- to _____

_____

- to _____

_____

MAGICAL PERFORMANCES:
getting the mundane and the magical things right

The activity where I want to deliver A magical performance is:

- _____

THE MUNDANE THINGS

The mundane things that must be done are:

- _____   - _____

- _____   - _____

- _____   - _____

The mundane things I must do personally are:

- _____   - _____

- _____   - _____

The things I can do to make these enjoyable or magical are:

- _____   - _____

- _____   - _____

The mundane things I can delegate are:

- _____   - _____

- _____   - _____

THE MAGICAL THINGS

The specific things I have done in the past to deliver magical performances are:

- _____

- _____

- _____

The specific things I can do to follow these patterns and produce magical performances in the future are:

- _____

- _____

- _____

The specific things I can add to my 'repertoire' to produce magical performances in the future are:

- _____

- _____

- _____

You can deliver success

'Great performances will eventually produce great results,' says Dave, the soccer manager. 'So my job is to educate the players to produce great performances. Football is big business, however, so I have made certain commitments to the Chairman. This season, my first in charge, we aim to finish in the top ten. Next year we aim to be in the top eight. The third year we aim to challenge for a place in Europe. Providing we do what works, both on and off the field, we will fulfil these promises.'

Robert Louis Stevenson wrote, 'To travel hopefully is a better thing than to arrive.' Nowadays employees recognise that you must also reach the destination. Sometimes the final push is required to gain the prize. Other times the prize arrives almost as a by-product, like an apple falling from a tree. Sounds odd? Perhaps, but if you have a putt on the final green to win the Ryder Cup, it is best to focus on the process, rather than worry about the hopes of a nation. Reaching the goal calls for balancing apparent paradoxes but, like Yin and Yang, these are often complementary. Balance The Spiritual Way with The Successful Way; The Beautiful Way with The Best Way; The Wise Way with The Winning Way. Satisfying sponsors is crucial. As Warren Bennis writes in *Organising Genius*, his study of superb groups, 'Great teams ship.'

You can focus on the next satisfying challenge

What to do after finishing? Winning the championship, writing the last page of a book or completing a project is exhilarating, but may give way to a sense of anti-climax. Suddenly the dominating drive in your life has vanished, to be replaced by a vacuum. Time to find a new purpose. Financially you might take an interim job to pay the mortgage, but the next step is crucial. Choose a challenge that you respect. Mountaineers always respect the mountain; otherwise they get into trouble. Falling into a project you do not respect leads to operating on cruise control and becoming sloppy. Allow yourself time to come through the change curve. Dare to relax, re-centre and then refocus. You will create a fresh purpose.

How to make this happen? You may wish to follow *The Satisfying Work Curve* (see illustration).

- Stage One is your **Seed Corn**. Exploring many possibilities in your life and work, you nurture the most fascinating interests, which leads to the next step.
- Stage Two is your **Satisfying Work**. You become obsessed with certain activities and find pursuing them extremely fulfilling, which leads to the next step.
- Stage Three is your **Salary Earner**. Translating the satisfying work into money-earning activities, you feel on top of the world. After a while you may want to move on, however, which leads to the final step.
- Stage Four is your **Spent Force**. The cash is still coming in, but performing the activities no longer generates energy. That does not matter, providing in the meantime you have been nurturing your next crop of Seed Corn, which continues the development cycle.

The satisfying work curve

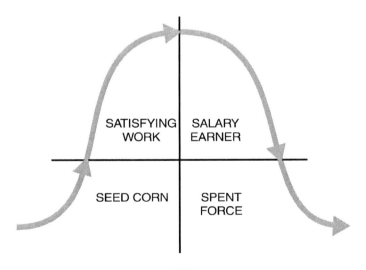

SATISFYING WORK | SALARY EARNER

SEED CORN | SPENT FORCE

Try tackling the exercise on this theme. Pay particular attention to turning your Satisfying Work into your next Salary Earner. Let's explore another way to translate your purpose into action.

SATISFYING WORK

MY SEED CORN
The things I can do to feed my seed corn are:

- _____
- _____
- _____

MY SATISFYING WORK
The things I can do to turn my satisfying work into my salary earner are:

- _____
- _____
- _____

MY SALARY EARNER
The things I can do to enjoy and capitalise on my salary earner are:

- _____
- _____
- _____

You can be a pacesetter

Pacesetters are different. They take the lead, maintain the lead and extend the lead. They make the new rules for the game. Some examples: Dick Fosbury created a new method of high jumping; Sony invented the Walkman; Abraham Maslow popularised the study of healthy people in psychology. People, teams and companies often follow five steps towards making breakthroughs in particular fields. They focus on their:

- **Passion**: they follow their passion.
- **Purpose**: they translate their passion into a clear purpose.
- **Professionalism**: they do highly professional work.
- **Peak Performance**: they achieve peak performance.
- **Pacesetting**: they make the new rules for the game.

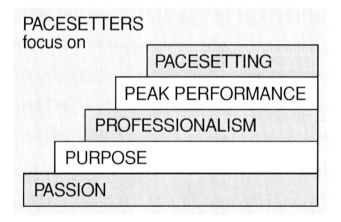

How to translate your passion into a purpose? Try tackling the exercise on this theme. First, write the name of somebody who showed this pioneering spirit. Second, describe what they did right to create the new rules. Third, describe what you can do to become – and remain – a Pacesetter. Such navigators venture into the darkness and chart the land for future generations. Is there an area where you can be a Pacesetter? Certainly we need the maps to help us build a positive planet.

PACESETTERS

This exercise invites you to do three things. First: to write the name of an individual, team or organisation that you believe has been a Pacesetter. Second: to describe what you believe they did right to be a Pacesetter in their chosen field. Third: to describe what you, your team or your business can do to become – and remain – a Pacesetter.

The Pacesetter's name (individual, team or organisation)

● _____

The things they did right to be a Pacesetter in their chosen field were:

● They _____

● They _____

● They _____

The things I can do to become - and remain - a Pacesetter are:

● _____

● _____

● _____

Conclusion

You never retire
from your vocation

Everybody has been granted a gift. If we are fortunate, loving parents, teachers and mentors enable us to follow this calling. Joseph Campbell talked about people pursuing *The Heroic Journey* towards the Holy Grail. For many of us, this is embodied in one of life's greatest adventures: 'Doing what we are here to do'. On one level this sounds simple, but it is not always straightforward. Much depends on when we learn to balance our soul work and salary work. Tackle the final exercise on this theme called *My Vocation*. Clarify how you can employ the right vehicles for continuing to do valuable work.

The Law of Return says: 'The things you give to the world are the things you get back from the world.' You reap what you sow. If you plant tomatoes, you will grow tomatoes, not carrots. If you encourage people, you will often receive encouragement in return. Take the ideas you like from this book and plant the seeds in your own way. Whatever harvest you reap, there will be other dreams to follow, other projects to pursue. One ending will bring new beginnings, because, 'You never retire from your vocation.'

MY VOCATION

VOCATION
I believe my vocation is:

- to _____

_____

VEHICLES
The vehicles I can employ to express my vocation are:

- _____

- _____

- _____

VALUABLE WORK
The valuable work I want to do is:

- to _____

- to _____

- to _____

Suggested Further Reading

The following books relate to following your vocation. Some titles have been mentioned in my previous books, but are included here to give an overview.

Christopher Alexander
THE TIMELESS WAY OF BUILDING
Oxford University Press – ISBN 0195024028 – 1979

An architect by profession, Christopher's ideas can be used in many fields of work. He declares: 'Each one of us has, somewhere in his heart, the dream to make a living world, a universe.' Architects believe that one day, somewhere, somehow, they will create a building that is wonderful, a place where people can walk and dream for centuries. Every person has some version of this dream. Some wish to create a house, a garden or a fountain. Others wish to create a relationship, a painting or other product. Christopher's book has relevance for anybody who wants to follow their calling.

Thomas Armstrong
7 KINDS OF SMART
Plume Books – ISBN 0452281377 – 1999

'Six years ago I quit my job as a learning disabilities specialist,' writes Thomas. 'I no longer believed in learning disabilities. It was then that I turned to the concept of learning differences as an alternative to learning disabilities.' Building on Howard Gardner's view of multiple intelligences, Thomas describes how each child is gifted in their own way. His book provides a treasure chest of ideas for enabling people to better use of the talents.

Warren Bennis and Patricia Ward Biederman
ORGANISING GENIUS: The Secrets Of Creative Collaboration
Nicholas Brealey Publishing – 1998

> What do great teams do right to perform exceptional work? 'Great groups start with great people. Great groups think they are on a mission from God. Great groups are full of talented people who can work together. Great groups make sure the right person has the right job. Great groups ship; they deliver the goods.' A fine book for anybody who wants to build a Super Team.

Bill Beswick
FOCUSED FOR SOCCER: Developing A Winning Mental Approach
Human Kinetics – ISBN 0736030026 – 2001

> Sounds an odd choice? Perhaps, but it is one of the best books on sports psychology and the lessons can be applied to any field of work. Bill provides tips and techniques that people can use to make the best use of their talents.

Richard Bolles
WHAT COLOUR IS YOUR PARACHUTE
Ten Speed Press – ISBN 089815880X – 1998

> Created over 30 years ago, the famous job-hunter's manual is now an annual best seller. Richard's approach to shaping your own destiny is now fully accepted, but his insights still provide much food for thought. A life-affirming book that is packed with fun cartoons and ideas for building a fulfilling future.

Marcus Buckingham & Don Clifton
NOW DISCOVER YOUR STRENGTHS
Simon & Schuster – 2001

> How do you perform World Class work? Surely it is by concentrating on 'improving' your weaknesses. Not so, say the authors: it is by learning how to leverage your talents. Marcus and Don are at the forefront of The Strengths Revolution. Packed with data, tools and ideas, this book shows how people can capitalise on what they do best.

Joseph Campbell & Diane K. Osborne (editor)
JOSEPH CAMPBELL COMPANION: Reflections On The Art Of Living
HarperCollins Publishers – 1991

Recorded during a seminar in California, Diane Osborn has weaved the themes together in a way that gives an overview of Joseph Campbell's work. The chapters cover such issues as relationships, 'following your bliss', spirituality and, of course, The Heroic Journey. Good to read in conjunction with Christopher Vogler's book, which is mentioned later.

Sheila Cassidy
SHARING THE DARKNESS
Darton, Longman and Todd Ltd. -1988

Sheila is the former Medical Director of St. Luke's Hospice in Plymouth. Listening to a patient, she reflects on her own life. 'I found myself saying again and again, 'You wash the feet that will not walk tomorrow', and realised that this was my job, my calling. I, who have little patience with the demented and no love for tiny babies, have a special gift of warmth and understanding for those whose time is running out. I, who hate parties and find it nigh impossible to make small talk know instinctively what to say and do for a gentle Manchester builder who is facing the humiliation of incontinence and the fear of death.' A thought-provoking book on following your purpose.

Mihaly Csikszentmihalyi
FLOW: The Psychology Of Optimal Experience
Perennial (HarperCollins) – 1991

Mihaly writes: 'We have all experienced times when, instead of being buffeted by anonymous forces, we do feel in control of our actions, masters of our own fate. On the rare occasions that it happens, we feel a sense of exhilaration, a deep sense of enjoyment that is long cherished and that becomes a landmark in memory for what life should be like. The best moments usually occur when a person's body or mind is stretched to its limits in a voluntary effort to accomplish something difficult and worthwhile. Optimal experience is therefore something that we make happen.' A fine book on feeling fully alive.

Viktor Frankl
MAN'S SEARCH FOR MEANING

Simon & Schuster – ISBN 0671023373 – 1997

Viktor describes his harrowing journey through the Nazi concentration camps. He found that many of the survivors had something to live for beyond the immediate terror. They had a book to write, a relationship to rebuild or a dream to pursue. He writes: 'Man is not free from his conditions, but he is free to take a stand towards his conditions.' As a result of his experiences, Viktor created a form of therapy that enabled people to fulfil their meaning in life.

Joline Godfery
IN OUR WILDEST DREAMS

HarperCollins – 1993

'Make Money, Have Fun, Do Good,' is the recipe for good work, says Joline. She describes the journey taken by many women who are running businesses. They want to combine quality of life with quality of work, rather than be forced to make a 'No Win' choice. One of the first books on the subject, it remains one of the best.

Paul Hawken
GROWING A BUSINESS

Simon & Schuster – 1987

Paul reached many budding entrepreneurs through his American Public Television series on this topic. He writes: 'Remember that in business you are never trying to 'beat' the competition. You are trying to give your customer something other than what they are receiving from the competition. It is a waste of time and energy trying to beat the competition because the customer doesn't care about that rivalry.' This practical book shows how to 'recreate something that has been lost' and use your imagination, rather than money, to achieve business success.

Eugen Herrigel
ZEN IN THE ART OF ARCHERY
Arkana – ISBN 0140190740 – 1988

Eugen spent several years in Japan attempting to learn this ancient art. Temptations took him off track before he was able to consistently release an arrow that hit the bulls-eye. He could then say: 'Bow, arrow, goal and ego, all melt into one another, so that I can no longer separate them. And even the need to separate has gone. For as soon as I take the bow and shoot, everything becomes so clear and straight forward and so ridiculously simple.' One of the first 'Zen In The Art Of....' books, this remains one of the most enlightening.

Barrie Hopson & Mike Scally
BUILD YOUR OWN RAINBOW
Management Books 2000 – ISBN 185252000X

This classic book, updated in 1999, takes the readers on a personal and professional journey. Packed with practical tools, it enables people to discover their work values, plus identify their occupational and transferable skills. Looking into the future, Rainbow helps readers to find their most comfortable career pattern and create action plans. It also offers a system for pursuing their personal development and finding courses built on the key themes outlined in the book.

Phil Jackson & Hugh Delehanty
SACRED HOOPS: Spiritual Journeys Of A Hardwood Warrior,
Hyperon – 1996

Phil Jackson is a former basketball coach of the Chicago Bulls championship winning team. He has a remarkable coaching philosophy, based on a mixture of Christianity, Zen and the Native American Indians. Well worth reading for an insight into how he got millionaire stars to submerge their egos and harness their talents into building a super team.

Richard J. Leider & David A. Shapiro
WHISTLE WHILE YOU WORK: Heeding Your Life's Calling
Berrett-Koehler – 2001.

> The authors offer many real-life examples of people who are following their vocation. They also provide an exercise entitled Calling Cards, which enables you to explore the themes that make up your unique contribution. Richard and David have a long track record of providing pioneering ways that people can use to translate their purpose into practice. You can access these ideas and books by visiting their website on: www.inventuregroup.com

Virginia Satir
THE NEW PEOPLEMAKING
Science & Behaviour Books – ISBN 0801400706 – 1988

> Virginia inspired many people with her pioneering approach to family therapy in the 1950s. Troubled parents often failed to communicate clearly, she said, and this led to suffering. The 'family pain' was then heaped on a 'problem child' or another family scapegoat. Her book contains wisdom and practical ideas that people can use to build healthy families.

Al Siebert
THE SURVIVOR PERSONALITY
HarperCollins – 1999

> What can we learn from survivors? Al Siebert identifies the characteristics of people who have overcome tremendous setbacks. Many of his findings, including the concept of Personal Radar, can be applied to our personal and professional lives. One of the best of the 'survivor' books on the market.

Christopher Vogler
THE WRITER'S JOURNEY: Mythic Structure For Storytellers & Screenwriters
Michael Wiese Productions – 1992

> Christopher's book shows how film plots often follow the structure that Joseph Campbell found in myths and legends. The

Heroic Journey is also followed by people who embark on their personal odyssey. Christopher writes: 'A hero leaves her comfortable, ordinary surroundings to venture into a challenging, unfamiliar world. It may be an outward journey to an actual place: a labyrinth, forest or cave, a strange city or country, a new locale that becomes the arena for her conflict with antagonistic, challenging forces ... But there are many stories that take the hero on an inward journey, one of the mind, the heart, the spirit. In any good story the hero grows and changes, making a journey from one way of being to the next: from despair to hope, weakness to strength, folly to wisdom, love to hate, and back again. It's these emotional journeys that hook an audience and make a story worth watching.' People may go through similar stages when pursuing their vocation.

Acknowledgements

Many people have provided the inspiration for *The Magic of Work*. My thanks go to:

- Sue Moore for her creative energy and breakthrough ideas in the area of Mentoring and Career Mentoring.
- Steve Harvey, Helen Duguid and all the people at Microsoft UK who have put the ideas into practice.
- Susanne Brealey for putting together the layout of the book.
- Everybody who has worked with me on following the Career Mentoring principles in their personal and professional lives.
- Nick Dale-Harris and James Alexander at Management Books 2000 for their belief and backing in publishing *The Magic of Work*.
- Charlotte Howard of Fox and Howard, literary agents, for her support.
- Berit, my wife, who continues to provide great encouragement.

Index

Endorsements

This book is a masterpiece of stimulating ideas that will enable people to flourish in the evolving world of work. It is full of questions that get to the heart of the issue and the heart of the person. Managers everywhere can use the tools to encourage people to do great work. Everybody can use the ideas to travel further on the journey towards achieving fulfilment in both their personal and professional lives.
Steve Harvey, Director of People, Profit and Loyalty,
Microsoft UK Ltd

Mike Pegg's genius for asking great questions takes the reader on a fascinating journey of self-challenge, self-discovery, reflection and release. For those who genuinely want to find deeper meaning and great fulfilment in work and in life – this book is a wonderful tool.
Jill Garrett, Principal European Consultant,
The Gallup Organization

The book gives an essential map to all of us striving to find our 'perfect role'. The Magic of Work is easy to follow and remarkably effective. It takes the mystery out of marrying your mission and your mortgage.
Simon Danciger, Director of E-Commerce
Freeserve

Incredibly practical and also inspiring. Many people want something more from life and work. This book provides the tools they can use to define and achieve their aims. I found the ideas extremely useful, both for my own development and that of my team.
Kate Lavender, Customer Service Director
AXA PPP Healthcare Ltd

The author asks fascinating questions that stimulate you to provide intriguing answers. The book is also packed with ideas that help you on the road towards doing stimulating work. Read the book. Do the exercises. Get the work you deserve

Chris Duckett, Managing Director
Duckett Accountants

One year ago, I set up my own business after spending many years working in organisations. I have found that the tools in this book are valuable to people wherever they apply their talents. The author gets right to the core of the issue facing so many of us – how to find a niche that allows us to flourish without it feeling like work!

Jane Hunt
JHC Consultancy Ltd

The Magic of Work is highly practical. It takes you through a series of great exercises and searching questions. The result can be the discovery of your own unique combination of soul work and salary work.

Sven Atterhed, Co-founder
The ForeSight Group

Very stimulating. The book provides a perfect opportunity for individuals to engage in a personal and career 'time-out' to reflect. It is full of valuable tools and exercises that really engage the reader.

Bill Beswick, Sports Psychologist and Assistant Manager
Middlesbrough Football Club

Today's organisations face the challenge of getting more from less. The best teams, sporting and business, are made up of people undertaking roles they love. How many of our people can we say that about? Mike's book shows us how to increase that number.

Roy White, General Manager, Human Resources
Sony Europe, Consumer Products